BYE BYE BLUES

For Alfred Emmet

BYE BYE BLUES
and other plays

James Saunders

AMBER LANE PRESS

All rights whatsoever in these plays are strictly reserved and
application for professional performance, etc., should be made
before rehearsal to:
Margaret Ramsay Ltd.,
14a Goodwin's Court,
St Martin's Lane,
London WC2N 4LL

Application for amateur performance should be made to:
Samuel French Ltd.,
26 Southampton Street,
London WC2E 7JE.

No performance may be given unless a licence has been
obtained.

First published in 1980 by
Amber Lane Productions Ltd.,
Amber Lane Farmhouse ,
The Slack,
Ashover, Derbyshire S45 0EB.

Printed in Great Britain by
A. Wheaton & Co. Ltd., Exeter.

Typesetting and make-up by
Computerset (Phototypesetting) Ltd., Oxford.

Copyright © James Saunders, 1980

ISBN 0 906399 13 0

Contents

BYE BYE BLUES

Characters

WOMAN 1
MAN 1
WOMAN 2
MAN 2
WOMAN 3
MAN 3

Bye Bye Blues was written for the Richmond Fringe and first performed by them at the Orange Tree Theatre, Richmond on 2 November, 1973. The cast was as follows:

WOMAN 1	Patricia Garwood
MAN 1	Bernard Holley
WOMAN 2	Isobil Nisbett
MAN 2	Paul Shelley
WOMAN 3	Pat Hope
MAN 3	Robert McBain

It was directed by Sam Walters.

There are three areas, within which are three women — WOMAN 1, WOMAN 2 and WOMAN 3 — and their men — MAN 1, MAN 2 and MAN 3. The style is cool, unemotional, matter-of-fact. In each area there is a table with a telephone and a bottle and two glasses.

WOMAN 1: I was standing by a shop window, waiting for somebody; I was late, they were not there, I was on the point of leaving. There was a display of equipment for eating out of doors; barbecues, metal garden furniture in various classical styles, sets of implements in stainless steel with rosewood handles. A notice said: *Design for Leisure.* I thought: 'How complex, how complex and expensive leisure is nowadays.' I heard my name called from across the road: 'Anne!' As I turned, there was a screech of brakes. I was too late to see what had happened. There was a car, stopped, on the other side of the road; another, level with it, was slewed across the road so that I couldn't tell even which way it had been going. The first driver got out and went round to the front of the car. Then I saw that someone was sitting in the road, as it seemed, almost in the gutter. My immediate thought was: 'Oh God, if they want a witness ... I saw nothing, I saw nothing ...' But then the pedestrian got up, seemed not to be hurt, perhaps had slipped, tripped in the gutter. They were talking to each other, they may have been arguing, or just excited, shocked. The second driver shouted something at them; they turned their heads, turning together, and stared at the driver leaning out through the car window, one arm and shoulder out. For a moment they were all three still, quite still, each in a particular stance as if posed: two heads turned, an arm raised from a car window, palm upturned, head jutting awkwardly out. I had then the sensation of a stillness persisting past its proper time, as if the tableau, three strangers caught in an accidental confrontation, had been chosen, fixed, selected for examination or display. And of course, myself watching them. As if someone, idly flicking through snapshots, had stopped, his attention caught by a particular one. Only through it, while they stood there still, a dog ran out from behind the cars and ran across the road, yelping. Its appearance was so sudden, so unexpected, that I turned and watched it until it disappeared up the street. Turning back to the three again, it seemed that they had still not moved, were still not moving; but then I saw that of course they were, were talking, arguing, raising their voices to each other. I found the episode oddly disturbing. I turned away; I was angry, I left them to sort it out as best they might, it was none of my business. My friend had not arrived, or gone already, I'd waited long enough. I walked back, to my car, and drove home. I was not expected.

WOMAN 2: Hello, what are you doing here?

MAN 2: I live here, don't you remember?

WOMAN 2: I thought you were to be out.

MAN 2: Yes, I was. I had a bit of a ... I missed my appointment.

WOMAN 2: Your *appointment*?

MAN 2: We missed each other.

WOMAN 2: Oh, I see. No, I don't see.

MAN 2: You're not really obliged to, are you?

WOMAN 2: No, of course not. All the same, if I'm talking to someone I like to be able to understand what they're talking about. Do you mind us talking?

MAN 2: Not at all.

WOMAN 2: Good, then we may as well make ourselves intelligible. And I don't know what you mean by having missed each other. Do you mean she wasn't there? Do you mean she didn't turn up?

MAN 2: I don't know whether she turned up or not.

WOMAN 2: Ah, then *you* didn't turn up.

MAN 2: Yes, I arrived.

WOMAN 2: You are being enigmatic, aren't you? Why don't you simply say you don't want to explain? Then I can

	leave it alone, it'll be a relief for us both. I don't want to pry.
MAN 2:	I don't mind explaining. It's rather mundane actually. I wouldn't have bored you with it. I'd almost got there and had a slight accident with the car.
WOMAN 2:	Oh?
MAN 2:	Nothing much, someone pulled over in front of me. Some fool ran into the road.
WOMAN 2:	Is the car all right?
MAN 2:	Yes, it was just a scratch, a scrape. I'm all right too.
WOMAN 2:	I can see you're all right. I couldn't see the car.
MAN 2:	A slight scratch on the wing, that's all. Not enough to claim for.
WOMAN 2:	Was his damaged?
MAN 2:	Hers.
WOMAN 2:	Oh. A woman driver. That explains it.
MAN 2:	A bent bumper. That was all we could see.
WOMAN 2:	You examined it together.
MAN 2:	Yes, together. Heads bowed together over the paint-work, examining it minutely, her hair brushing mine, fingers tracing gently a tiny scratch, first my finger, then hers.
WOMAN 2:	Hm.
WOMAN 3:	Nobody was hurt?
MAN 3:	No, no . . .
WOMAN 3:	That was good.
MAN 3:	You're going out?
WOMAN 3:	Yes, I shall be. Are you, again?
MAN 3:	I don't know. I don't suppose so. Not now.
WOMAN 3:	Only I thought I might use the car, since it's back; if you're not going out.
MAN 3:	Yes, certainly.
WOMAN 3:	I don't want to rob you of it. Constrict you.
MAN 3:	You've as much right to it as I have.
WOMAN 3:	After all, I'd have had to take the bus, I'm quite prepared to.
MAN 3:	Take the car, I shan't need it.
WOMAN 3:	I would prefer. I don't like buses. Relying on other

people's timetables and routes. Having to wait, having to walk. And unreliable, of course; other people are. One's so much freer in a car. One can change one's mind, make sudden decisions. I'll take it then. What are you going to do?

MAN 3:   I don't know. Watch television. I might ring someone up.

          [*The phone rings.*]

          Or be rung up. Hello . . . I'm sorry . . .? I'm sorry, you have the wrong number. This is 9523 . . . No, she isn't. There's no-one of that name here.

MAN 2:   We'd had a stupid argument, one of the usual. I said she could do as she damned well liked. She slammed out of the house. I heard her car start, grinding the gears. I put down a stiff whisky, got in my car, and drove off. I was to meet someone, I was late on account of the stupid argument. We're free people, adults, I don't know why we have such arguments. On the way there was a bit of an accident, nothing serious, though it could have been. By the time things were sorted out they were gone. Or hadn't turned up. I drove home, angry and disturbed.

MAN 1:   So you'll stay in now?

WOMAN 1: Yes. Cut my losses.

MAN 1:   Have an evening in, why not?

WOMAN 1: You're off are you, to wherever you're going?

MAN 1:   Yes. Why?

WOMAN 1: Nothing. Purely selfish. I don't want to be in on my own.

MAN 1:   Have someone in; ring someone up.

WOMAN 1: Hm . . . Perhaps I shall.

MAN 1:   You've plenty of friends.

WOMAN 1: Yes, I probably shall, when you've gone.

MAN 1:   Why wait till then? They'll all be fixed up, all be out for the evening.

WOMAN 1: So long as you don't change your mind. You have been known to.

MAN 1:   I *have* to go out, I'm sorry.

WOMAN 1: That's all right. I'm not asking you to stay in. You're free to do as you like.

MAN 1: I told you, I'm not; I've arranged to meet someone, I can't break it now.

WOMAN 1: I'm not asking you to. Only you didn't tell me you'd arranged to meet someone.

MAN 1: I said I had to go. Why else would I have to go out?

WOMAN 1: Because you want to.

MAN 1: As a matter of fact I don't, particularly. I'd just as soon stay in. If I'd known you'd be in, I'd have kept the evening free.

WOMAN 1: How was I to know I'd be in? Stupid accident . . . not that it's important.

MAN 1: It's obviously important if you —

WOMAN 1: Oh please don't say it. You're taking the car?

MAN 1: Yes.

WOMAN 1: The bumper's bent. Nothing much.

WOMAN 2: And so you were late for your appointment.

MAN 2: I was late in any case. I'd been held up by a — oh, a stupid argument with someone.

WOMAN 2: At the office? So you drove off angrily, late for your meeting, and had an accident.

MAN 2: You mean it was my fault.

WOMAN 2: I didn't say that at all.

MAN 2: Of course you didn't. You never do. You put two statements together which imply a certain con-clusion. Then you dissociate yourself from the con-clusion; as if it hadn't occurred to you. Why don't you say what you think, instead of playing games? It's simpler.

WOMAN 2: Is that what you want, simplicity? I'd hate to bore you with my mundane thoughts, when were you in-terested in what I think? I didn't say it hadn't occurred to me, of course it occurred to me that you were the cause of this — ineffectual accident you had. Somebody was the cause, you or somebody else or both. And you were angry, and therefore more likely to go over the top, misjudge a situation.

MAN 2: She was angry too, as far as I could tell. The other driver.

WOMAN 2: At you? Perhaps you made her angry.

MAN 2: Or perhaps she was angry in the first place.

WOMAN 2: Yes. Perhaps. Perhaps she was late for an appointment. Perhaps she'd had a stupid row.

MAN 2: I was going too fast, I agree, a little too fast. I was in a hurry. Why don't you take your coat off?

WOMAN 2: I'm going out. Just waiting for a call. So when you'd got there, she'd gone.

MAN 2: I don't know whether she'd gone or not. I don't know whether she'd come.

WOMAN 2: Why don't you ring her up?

> [*He considers this for a moment, then does so. He listens, then puts the phone down.*]

Out?

MAN 2: Engaged.

WOMAN 2: She's probably ringing you.

WOMAN 1: Yes, I shall ring up a friend or two. Perhaps watch a little television, there's a programme I'd not mind seeing. Spontaneity has become, though — have you noticed — ? — a little ... difficult. A rare commodity. Now that we order our lives so well, now that we have such freedom. Allow each other such freedom. One pays for everything, I suppose. Spontaneity with other people, I mean, making a casual arrangement on a whim, on the spur of the moment, because one wants to do something with someone *now*, not in a week's time or a month's time ... On one's own it's easy enough: I look in my diary, find a blank space, an empty evening, and there, I can be as spontaneous as I like, on my own, I'm free, though it usually comes down to a mooning about, a leafing through magazines, a watching of television. We've become like football teams, don't you think? We arrange our fixtures at the beginning of the season. And woe betide us if some accident upsets them. I'm not sure it's an ideal arrangement.

MAN 1: How else can one operate?

WOMAN 1: Operate? Operate what?

MAN 1: Life, one's life.

WOMAN 1: Like a machine, you mean, as one operates a machine, a car? Perhaps that's the trouble: we don't live any more, we've given up living, much too casual and messy. Instead, we operate our lives. We sit at the controls. Only we don't believe in controls any more, do we? We believe in freedom, freedom to do as one wants. But how does one control a free machine?

MAN 1: Look, I'll stay in if you wish; break the appointment.

WOMAN 1: Good God, no. What are you thinking of?

MAN 1: I don't particularly want to go.

WOMAN 1: So you'll stay with me. Thank you, no.

[She picks up the phone and dials.]

Hello . . . Yes. I happen to be free this evening . . . No, an accident, a stupid accident. Nothing serious. I wondered if *you* were free, by any chance . . . Yes, of course . . . No, no, no . . . Bless you.

[She puts the phone down. He looks at her but she gives nothing away.]

WOMAN 2: My attention was diverted, I took my eyes off the road for a second. I was late, I was driving too fast, not in the best of moods. Someone called out, I thought it was my name: 'Anne!' I glanced round, thought I saw him, there was a screeching of brakes, a car was in my path, a pedestrian in the road, a dog; I braked, instinctively wrenched the wheel . . . !

MAN 3: When are you going?

WOMAN 3: Soon. Why?

MAN 3: No reason.

WOMAN 3: Are you waiting to ring someone?

MAN 3: Why should I wait till you've gone?

WOMAN 3: I don't know. You're free.

MAN 3: As you are.

WOMAN 3: But one likes one's secrets, I suppose, even if they're not necessary. One isn't always entirely rational.

MAN 3: There's no-one I particularly want to ring up. If there were, I'd ring them.

WOMAN 3: You'll want to explain why you missed your appointment.

MAN 3: Yes, I suppose so.

WOMAN 3: She may be waiting there still.

MAN 3: I told you, I arrived, finally.

WOMAN 3: Oh yes, and she was gone.

MAN 3: Or hadn't come.

WOMAN 3: She'd not let you down, surely.

MAN 3: Why not? People do.

WOMAN 3: Hm.

MAN 3: I only asked when you were going because I find it a little unsettling when someone's getting ready to go somewhere. That's all.

WOMAN 3: Disturbing?

MAN 3: Unsettling. I feel called upon in some way.

WOMAN 3: You're not called upon. There's nothing I want of you, you're free.

MAN 3: I know. It's irrational. But I can't settle down till you've gone.

WOMAN 3: I'm not going for a few minutes. Not if I'm taking the car.

MAN 3: I'm not trying to push you out.

WOMAN 3: I thought dogs weren't allowed on main roads, without a lead.

MAN 3: They're not by rights. The dogs don't always realise that.

[*The phone rings.*]

MAN 2: Hello ... Anne ...? What happened ...? No, I was late ... Nothing much ... No, I can't now. I have to go out ... Next week ...? So sorry. Bless you.

WOMAN 3: You might have been killed.

MAN 3: Hm?

WOMAN 3: Mightn't you? Because of that dog.

MAN 3: It wasn't only the dog. I thought I saw a friend across the road, I was careless.

WOMAN 3: It was the dog made the car swerve, you said.

MAN 3: The car was going too fast. But I agree, I could have been killed. Or *might* have been killed. Because of a peculiar combination of events. Not even peculiar. A random coming together of carlessnesses.

WOMAN 3: What a word.

MAN 3: Errors of judgement ... Yes, I might have been killed. Because, for instance, someone, some stranger, let the dog out by mistake, stormed out of the house, perhaps after a row, let the dog escape.

WOMAN 3: Do you really think it's as accidental as that?

MAN 3: What else?

MAN 1: We are not responsible for one another.

WOMAN 1: Who said we were? I didn't.

MAN 1: There's an implication, isn't there?

WOMAN 1: Is there?

MAN 1: That I am in some way responsible for the fact that, because of an accident which was no fault of mine, you are having to stay at home alone while I go out.

WOMAN 1: What on earth are you on about? You're free. I'm asking nothing of you. So long as you ask nothing of me. Leave me alone, then, keep your implications to yourself.

MAN 2: My eyes were off the road, someone had called out, I swerved to avoid the dog, then back as a car slewed round in front of me, I swerved again, braked hard, thought: 'My God, I'm going to hit her!'

MAN 3: What if I had been?

WOMAN 3: What if you had been what?

MAN 3: Killed. If I'd been killed, what would you do?

WOMAN 3: What a strange question. What could I do? Mourn you, I suppose; grieve for you. What else?

MAN 3: And then what?

WOMAN 3: How do I know? What do you mean? I couldn't bring you to life, could I, whatever I did? I must go now or I shall be late. You think you'd be forgotten, is that what you mean? You think you'd go unnoticed, leave nothing?

MAN 3: What would I leave?

WOMAN 3: What would any of us leave? What would *I* leave? What is it you want? You weren't killed. What do you want?

[*The phone rings.*]

Hello ... No ... I'm sorry, you've got the wrong number.

[*She puts the phone down.*]

What is it you want?

[MAN 1 *has dialled.*]

MAN 1: Hello . . . No, I wanted to speak to Anne . . . Out . . .? Would you tell her . . . No, it doesn't matter. I may ring again.

MAN 2: I wonder you bother to ask all these questions.

WOMAN 2: Hm?

MAN 2: Whether I saw who I was to see, whether . . . These expressions of concern.

WOMAN 2: Why should I not be concerned? You'd rather I were not?

MAN 2: You're not. Interested, I suppose, vaguely, if you've nothing else on your mind; not concerned. For me?

WOMAN 2: You'd like me to be? You think I should be? You need my concern? Very well, I'm interested in what you do, why should I not be? Is there something you'd like me not to know, are you afraid I shall find something out, is that what's bothering you?

MAN 2: Nothing's bothering me. Why should I bother to have secrets from you?

WOMAN 2: Why indeed? You're free. You can do as you like.

MAN 2: As you can.

WOMAN 2: And if I do ask questions, which you're loath to answer, I notice, that's more to the point, I should say, not why I ask questions but why you make such heavy weather answering them — if I do ask questions, do express some interest in what you do, which is more than *you* do, I think there's reason enough for it in the fact that we do live together, are in some kind of way linked to each other, responsible to each other.

MAN 2: Responsible to each other?

WOMAN 2: You don't think so! You find the idea strange?

MAN 2: Frankly, yes. To hear you say it, to hear you talk of responsibility. Who was so obsessed with freedom, with keeping her freedom —

WOMAN 2: As you were.

MAN 2: Well, and you have it; and so have I. You use it, and so do I. It's as you wanted it. As we both wanted it. We are free. And now you're talking about responsibility? What is it you want now? That I should be — ?

WOMAN 2: Nothing, I want nothing! I want nothing from you! Do as you like!

MAN 3: ... thinking I saw her across the road, in front of a shop window; called out: 'Anne!' She turning, stepping into the road, as I did; a screeching of brakes, a car between us, another slewing round, tyres screeching; 'My God,' I thought, 'she's hit' ...

WOMAN 1: Do as you damned well like.

MAN 1: You think it's as simple as that? You think we're that independent?

WOMAN 1: Are we not? You operate your life, I operate mine, isn't that the way of it?

MAN 1: Then why are we bothering to argue with each other?

WOMAN 1: Let's not, then. It's not my idea, get in your car and go, go and keep your appointment, for God's sake.

MAN 1: And forget you?

WOMAN 1: Of course. Why not?

MAN 1: And you'll forget me?

WOMAN 1: Yes. Immediately.

MAN 1: Want nothing of me, expect nothing of me?

WOMAN 1: No. Nothing.

MAN 1: Not even that I come back?

WOMAN 2: We got out of our cars, this stranger and I, inspected the damage together. We stooped together to examine the damage: nothing much, a slight scratch on a wing, a dented bumper. I ran my finger along the scratch, he did the same, casually, intently, saying nothing, we said nothing. My hair brushed his face; two strangers. Then I looked up, and saw the pedestrian, in the road ...

MAN 1: Not even that I come back?

WOMAN 1: Hm? What?

MAN 1: Do you care if I come back? Do you want me to come back?

WOMAN 1: What does it matter what I want?

MAN 1: It matters if I'm asking.

WOMAN 1: What difference does it make? You'll do as you like.

MAN 1: As you do. I'm asking you a question. Why the hell don't you answer?

WOMAN 1: I'm not going to interfere with your freedom. I'm not
going to be accused of interfering with your freedom!
You're free, do as you damned well like.

MAN 1: All right, then. Have it your own way. To hell with it!
[*He leaves. The phone rings.*]

WOMAN 1: Hello . . . Yes, I am, as it happens . . . Where . . .? Yes,
all right . . . See you then. Bless you.
[*She puts the phone down.*]

WOMAN 3: I must go. I shall be late. What is it that you want?
What are you trying to say?

MAN 3: We're free people, independent; we go our own way.
How can we mourn one another if we're free? How
can we be free if we'd mourn one another? Why
should you grieve for me?

WOMAN 3: Why? You ask why?

MAN 3: How, then? What sudden change of heart would it
be? For us to mourn one another?

WOMAN 3: I'm afraid I've no idea what —
[*The phone rings.* WOMAN 3 *takes it.*]
Hello . . . Yes . . . Yes, I'm on my way!
[*She puts the phone down.*]
I must go.

MAN 3: Regret I can understand. We'd regret the loss of one
another. One regrets losing what one has grown used
to. A particular possession, a particular person.

WOMAN 3: You think that's all? That's all it is for you?

MAN 3: Grief is another matter, mourning, which comes so
glibly off your tongue, is another matter. What have
we given one another, that the loss of it would be in-
supportable? We've arrived at a working arrangement; we live together, we have our own lives. We're
free, we have no holds on one another, make no
assumptions, no demands, ask nothing but cool
tolerance, to be allowed. When we happen to . . .

WOMAN 3: [*over*] I *have* to go.

MAN 3: . . . be together, there's the easy comfort of familiarity,
a relaxation, a rest from whatever it is we're after.
When we're apart, there's nothing.

WOMAN 3: [*over*] You want never to be out of my mind, is that it,
never for an instant?

MAN 3: While I was out we were dead to one another. Less than dead, death implies memories, there were no memories. If I'd been killed, taken suddenly out, think what you'd gain: you'd be quite free then; and be able to think of me, remember me, with affection, without danger, without hurt.

WOMAN 3: I've got to go. I'm late now. You're talking nonsense. I shall have to take this away with me now. I suppose that's what you wanted. Damn you.

> [WOMAN 3 *leaves.*]

WOMAN 2: When it began, there seemed no reason why it should end. It was self-sufficient. It supplied its own needs, fed on itself, replenished and refreshed itself, looked only inwards, was its own world. Then came a lack, a dissatisfaction, becoming a hunger, a starving; our world was dying of hunger. We compromised, we made the best we could, thinking it was for the best. We went our own ways; we stayed together. We thought: after all, we are together; we are moving with the times; we are free, we must be free, together but free. We have lost something. We have cheated somewhere. Cheated one another. When I talk of responsibility, it's that that I mean. And when I show interest in things which are not, it seems, my concern, it's only perhaps that in examining the surface of our lives I'm hoping for some meaning, something that means something. Or perhaps, of course, simply whiling away the time.

> [WOMAN 2 *stands, looking at* MAN 2. MAN 3 *has dialled a number. Phone 2 rings.* WOMAN 2 *takes it.*]

Hello.

MAN 3: Hello ... Anne?

WOMAN 2: Who is it you want?

MAN 3: Look, I'm free.

WOMAN 2: I'm sorry, you have the wrong number.

MAN 3: Shall we meet ...? As soon as you like.

WOMAN 2: This is 9523, I'm afraid there's no-one of that name here.

> [*She puts the phone down.*]

MAN 3: See you then. Bless you.

> [*He puts the phone down and leaves.* WOMAN 2 *looks for a moment longer at* MAN 2 *and leaves.*]

MAN 2: I left late, disturbed and angry; put down a stiff scotch and left. I felt constricted, put upon. I drove fast, as if to escape; there was nothing to escape from, I was free. Someone caught my attention, standing on the other side of the road, waiting for somebody, I suppose; just a glimpse, but I was held by it. I knew that I would remember her for the rest of my life; and that we would never meet. I thought: 'There is my true fate, which I have missed; I am driving past it; it will never come again.' At that moment she stepped into the road, as if she had seen someone she knew; there was a screeching of brakes, a car was in my path, skidding. I thought: 'This is it, this is it . . .'

> [*He takes a drink and leaves.* WOMAN 1 *has listened to him. Now she listens as the sound comes of cars, the screeching of brakes and tyres, a collision. She leaves.*]

THE END

THE ISLAND

A Male Chauvinist Comedy

Characters

The sisters:
KAY
SUE, the youngest
JO
VI
DEE

The brothers:
POD, the younger
MAT

The Island was written for and first performed by the Questors
Theatre, Ealing, in June 1975. The cast was as follows:

KAY	Lorna Duval
SUE	Caroline O'Reilly
JO	Jo Arundel
DEE	Helen Blatch
VI	Sheila Tiffany
POD	Tony Barber
MAT	David Gower

It was directed by Robin Duval.

The first professional production was by the Richmond Fringe at
the Orange Tree Theatre, Richmond, on 21 January, 1977. The
cast was as follows:

KAY	Patricia Brake
SUE	Julie Neesam
JO	Ruth Goring
DEE	Helen Blatch
VI	Isobil Nisbett
POD	Geoffrey Beevers
MAT	Mark Jones

It was directed by Roger Swaine.

*A clearing on a semi-tropical island. A rude hut is
visible. Exotic bird noises.* KAY *enters.*

KAY: Toward the end of the twentieth century, as the last
lights of the last of the wars of men flickered across the
depopulated wastes and wreckage of the world like the
last sparks of a fire having nothing left to burn, the
women survivors, savages now, stripped to the bare
bones of survival-lust and hate-lust, turned on their
men returning contaminated, weakened from battle
and, first one, then more, then all, killed and ate them.
Thus began the new age of woman. Then, too, as if as a
token of nature's blessing on a new order of things, the
first child was born of woman only, no man having had
access. A girlchild this, as all those following; no more
menchildren were born, or, if they were, they were dis-
posed of. Our mother was the first of that new breed of
unsired young; she, too, had children, girlchildren, five
in number, of no man; as shall, in our time, we. Then,
leaving her native place, she brought us here, to this
deserted isle, to see us begin, before she died, a new life
of peace and harmony. So much for the past; hear now
our play.
[SUE *enters.* KAY *exits.*]
SUE: Oh, sisters, how good it is to be alive in the world.
[JO *and* DEE *enter.*]
JO: And on such a morning.
DEE: Yes, indeed.
[*They respond to* SUE*'s innocent and heartfelt
exclamation in a manner not altogether con-
vincing, as if their minds were on other things.*]
SUE: Last night I dreamt I rode on the back of a fabulous
winged creature, strong yet gentle. We flew together
above the clouds with the speed of the wind, yet the air
caressed my body as tenderly as, as — as a summer
breeze blowing off warm seas, while the sun pierced me
gently. To marvellous places my creature took me,
where we lay amongst fragrant grasses eating delicious

wild-growing fruits until I cried with pleasure and
woke, still crying at the beauty of it. Yet I was not tired
or sated but refreshed by my night's journeyings and
pleasurings. I woke to the sun playing on my face, the
call of a bird trilling its contentment high in the sky,
the sweet lush sound of waves washing the sand. And I
thought: this must surely be another dream. I have
woken from a dream so real that I cried with pleasure,
to a reality so like a dream that I must laugh with
delight that I live in a world that provides night and
day such bounty. And as I sat up and saw the sweet
sleeping faces of my sisters, it seemed for a moment that
this was indeed a dream from which I must wake, that
reality could not, nor was meant, to be so sweet, so
simple, that darker journeyings lay ahead on another,
colder creature, a creature hard as steel to whose back I
must some day commit myself. But then I came to
myself again and shook off my fears.

> [*Pause.*]

DEE: Whose turn to make breakfast?

JO: Yours.

DEE: Is it?

JO: Vi Monday, me Tuesday —

DEE: I'll take your word for it.

> [*Pause.*]

Right.

> [*She looks at the sky.*]

Not going to rain again today.

JO: Doesn't look like it.

DEE: Hasn't rained since we arrived.

JO: Who needs rain?

DEE: Well exactly. A spring of first-class water, cold as a
mountain-top and gin-clear. And the plant life seems
to manage perfectly well; very luscious, loaded with
juicy fruits. Who needs rain?

JO: Same old blue, day after day, not a cloud in the sky . . .

SUE: There are clouds.

JO: Where?

SUE: There, look. Fans and streamers of white, look, high up

where even the birds never reach. As if someone took a
brush and decorated the sky just for the fun of it.

DEE: What fun!

[*Pause.*]

It won't rain. It'll never rain here. I've got a feeling. It's
found a way to do without.

JO: So we don't need it.

DEE: Very lucky we don't need it. If we did, we'd be unlucky.

[*Pause.* SUE *looks up at the sky.*]

SUE: It seems to me sometimes —

DEE: *Fruit* for breakfast?

JO: Whatever we've got.

DEE: We've got fruit. Five different kinds of fruit. And wild
honey gathered from the hives of friendly bees, who
build their hives, it seems, always at shoulder-height in
the trunks of trees and have never been known to sting.

JO: Not yet.

DEE: They've probably got no sting.

JO: Wild honey would be lovely.

DEE: Right.

[*Pause. She looks round for something to give
her attention to.*]

I'll off and do it then.

SUE: I'll come and help.

DEE: No. Thanks.

[DEE *exits.*]

SUE: It seems to me sometimes —

JO: Have you cleaned your teeth?

SUE: Why do you ask me every morning if I've cleaned my
teeth? You know we don't have to clean our teeth here.

JO: That's true, I forgot.

SUE: Every morning you forget.

JO: Disease is unknown here. Teeth stay sound and white
through the action of fruit and the wild honey which
we constantly eat.

SUE: And the soft white bark of the bread-bark tree.

JO: And the delicious soft white bark of the bread-bark tree,
how could I forget.

SUE: How happy I am this morning.

JO: Good.

SUE: Listen, I want to ask you something . . . What are you looking at?

JO: You've got better eyes than I have.

SUE: Over there? On the beach? [*She shades her eyes.*] Only our sister Vi. Standing looking at — something. On the sand . . . Stooping to it now and . . . Now she's walking away, walking fast away. I wonder what it is. Some dead thing . . .? When I woke this morning, for instance, why did I think I was waking into a dream? Because I'm happy? Happiness is real, unhappiness is the dream. We are part of nature, we are made to be content. There was a bird, high in the sky, singing its heart out, high thin notes like silver needles. I closed my eyes and it became a pain. I lay like this on the grass and let myself be pierced by the pain of those silver needles . . . Shall I gather some flowers?

JO: Why not?

SUE: I'll do that.

JO: Do. [*She watches* SUE *exit.*] She's a good child. If she didn't talk such rubbish. Twelve months we have sojourned on this sunny isle, made it our home. Though it could be twelve years, or days. An even, balmy clime, a full moon every night, believe it or not, and day by day the same waves lap on the same sands, each no bigger or smaller than the last. Unblemished fruit stands on the tree — trees, offers itself from a comfortable arm's length, and as one plucks it more appears. Or so it seems; it's a profligate island. No fairies here, but there is a kind of tree grows a little higher than the others, its branches of a particular vibrant wood; when the breeze catches them in a special way they make music; sweet, unworldly music which smooths the brow, soothes the senses, and lulls the listener into a dreamy languor; sometimes it goes on for days, when the wind's in the right direction. Then we lie, faces to the sun, or moon, chewing slowly the incredible flesh of the fruit of heaven, as we call it, high as kites on ethereal vibrations. The wind at the moment, thank God, has dropped.

[*Pause.*]
On the mainland all was progressing favourably under the new order. War was unknown, of course, since we'd dispensed with the causers of it. There were, however, certain lapses, certain disappointments; old habits die hard, even when learned at second hand. Difficulties were put down to male residues; masculine characteristics of appearance or behaviour were frowned on as deviationist; we watched ourselves, and each other. A woman grew a moustache and was severely beaten. With our mother we took ship and landed on this uninhabited but hospitable isle; where we live, as I say, a life others might envy. Shall I go now and pick some flowers? No, I'll wait for my sister, who I see now hurrying towards me from the shore. She comes to tell us of the discovery she had made while searching for pretty shells: the bodies of two creatures who, from certain characteristics, I can only presume to have been men. There, at the sea's edge. I know, because I found them first.

> [*She looks out, waiting for* VI *to arrive.* DEE *enters from the hut with plates of fruit, etc.*]

DEE: Breakfast.

> [*She slaps the stuff down on the table and goes back in for more.*]

JO: I hoped they'd go away.

> [KAY *enters. She comes across to join* JO. DEE *enters with drinks.*]

DEE: Milk of the mutated coconut, which ferments of itself in the shell, producing a rather cheeky young wine, slightly sparkling, goes well with fruit and wild honey. Try it with the bark of the bread-bark tree. What are you looking at?

KAY: See how slowly she comes, with faltering step, biting her lip the while and casting ever and again a backward glance, whether of regret or fear one cannot tell. What can it be that she has found?

JO: A couple of bodies.

DEE: Bodies?

JO: Since she's such a long time getting here.

DEE: Bodies of what?

JO: Men.

DEE: I thought you said men.

JO: I did.

> [DEE *takes a drink of coconut milk.*]

KAY: Oh, horror!

JO: That's one way of looking at it.

DEE: How do you know?

JO: I was having my morning swim, wasn't I?

DEE: You didn't tell us.

JO: Nobody asked.

DEE: And you just left them there?

JO: I thought they'd go away.

DEE: How can they if they're dead?

JO: The tide . . .

DEE: There's no tide.

JO: Or something. I don't know.

DEE: How do you know they're men?

JO: I put two and two together. You can't see from here.

> [VI *enters.*]

VI: Oh, sisters, I have strange news —

DEE: Breakfast is on the table.

JO: Where are you going?

DEE: For a swim.

> [DEE *exits.*]

VI: Strange news, sisters. As I was —

JO: We know, I've done it. She can't swim.

VI: You've seen them?

JO: She hates the water, says the salt makes her itch. Yes.

VI: What are we to do?

JO: I don't know. Bury them, I suppose.

VI: We can't do that.

JO: Why not, the sand's soft enough.

VI: Alive?

JO: What do you mean alive? They're not alive.

VI: They're alive.

JO: Rubbish.

VI: Oh horror.

JO: Do shut up, You're mistaken. They're dead.

VI: One of them turned his head, so.

JO: Rigor mortis.

VI: I felt their hearts beat.

JO: You what?

VI: Strangely flat and hard their chests, lightly covered with hair, one more than the other. Warm. And the hearts beat softly . . .

JO: You have been researching, haven't you?

VI: I washed my hands after.

KAY: Oh horror.

> [*She begins to go.*]

JO: You come back. Someone better blow the alarm.

> [KAY *goes to the conch-shell hanging outside the hut and blows it. There is an answering chorus of jungle noises.*]

VI: So you saw them too.

JO: Yes.

VI: Did you . . .?

> [KAY *blows again.*]

JO: That'll do.

KAY: I'll go and find Sue.

> [KAY *exits.*]

JO: Did I what?

VI: Did you feel anything?

JO: What are you getting at?

VI: When you saw them, when you looked at them. Did you feel anything?

JO: I don't know what you mean. Did you feel anything — apart from their chests?

VI: No. No, no, no. Nothing.

> [*Pause.*]

JO: Nothing?

VI: Well —

JO: Yes?

VI: I must say, to be honest, as I stood there looking at these two strange objects washed ashore — presumably . . .

JO: I suppose.

VI: Lying so still, one curled like an unborn child, the other, the older one, stretched out, arms flung so, as if crucified on the sand, defenceless, defeated . . .

JO: You must say what?

VI: My feelings were mixed . . . I knew what I should feel
about these creatures, these organisms, as one feels
about a plague germ. I remembered what I'd been
taught, images passed through my mind, highlights
from the history of man, images of cruelty, destruc-
tion, the wasting of the world for useless purposes. I
knew what I should feel and knew, too, what it would
be best to do, best for all: pull them, first one then the
other, by the feet, back down into the sea that threw
them up.

JO: Alive?

VI: I even picked up the feet of one of them, the younger,
only as I began to drag him his body straightened and
the head rolled over, so . . . And the hearts beat just like
other hearts . . .

[DEE *enters.*]

DEE: I've got news for you.

JO: We know.

DEE: Well? Isn't somebody going to do something?

[*She goes purposefully to the conch and blows
it. No sound comes out.*]

Oh, well, we shall all be murdered where we stand then,
that's obvious. It's only a matter of time. Sweet reason
versus brute force, the mindless beast let loose in the
arena, it's a foregone conclusion. I wonder if it's worth
having breakfast first.

JO: We haven't even got a gun.

VI: We don't believe in guns.

JO: Even if we did, we haven't got one, have we? I bet they
believe in guns.

VI: Perhaps they'll leave us alone.

DEE: Can you give me one case in the history of humanity
when men were content to leave things alone? When
they came uninvited into somebody else's territory and
left them alone?

VI: Erm . . .

DEE: Don't bother.

JO: Listen, if we took a big sort of — branch or something
. . .

[*She goes to the conch and holds it awkwardly
in her hands like a club.*]

If we — if we went down there now, before they come
to. And, and, hit them on the, on the head, like that —

[*She demonstrates, raising the conch above her
head with both hands and bringing it down
smartly. Only, of course, because of the rope
from which it hangs it jumps out of her hands
and swings wildly about her head. She ducks
and shrieks.*]

DEE: Any other ideas?

VI: They won't necessarily — hurt us, will they? Do you
think?

JO: Oh, no. Not necessarily.

DEE: Perhaps unnecessarily.

JO: Or only to start with, to show us who's in charge. I
expect they'll find five of us rather more than they need.
They'll get rid of one or two of us, commit a few
atrocities of one kind and another and throw the bodies
into the sea. They won't hurt the rest of us, or only if
they feel like it, they do sometimes get a bit of fun out of
hurting people but only for recreation, nothing serious
intended. One thing about them, they do realise the
value of human life, if they own it. Maybe they'll just
dispose of one of us, not Sue, they like young ones, one
of us three I should think, and still own two of us each,
a nice controllable number. Quite a status symbol we'll
be, as well as doing their work for them. Not that much
work needs doing here, where all the necessities are
provided for, but they'll think something up. After all,
what's the point of owning slaves if there's nothing to
make them do? They'll start making changes, rational-
ise the island, put it on a proper economic footing. Cut
down unnecessary trees, clear the undergrowth, cement
over half the island, build some offices for administra-
tion, we'll do all that. Then they can set about making
the place economically viable, export surplus fruit,
we'll have to tighten our belts a bit of course, to help
things along, the less we eat the more we can export;

and then what about a bit of light industry, there's not much money in fruit and honey. We'll need to increase the population, provide workers for industry, patriotic duty. And buy things, buy the things we make; no point making things if you don't buy them, and you've got to have a firmly based home market. Nice washing machines, things like that, labour-saving devices, to give us more time to work in the factories making washing machines. I can see great things happening to this island; we'll become a power to be reckoned with, a great power. We'll need protecting from our enemies, envious eyes abroad. What about an army then? Good idea, great consumers, armies, good things to have around. You're not respected till you're feared and you're not feared till you've got yourself an army. Then, of course, there's the matter of a king, we'll need a king, someone to look up to, crystallise our aspirations, someone to fight for. No, they won't hurt us, not necessarily, not if we behave ourselves.

[*Pause.*]

Help!

SCENE TWO

A bit of beach. On it lie two men, dressed in castaway's
uniform: baggy shirts, raggedy trousers and bare feet.
They lie for a while, motionless. Then the sound of the
conch-shell is heard from a little way off and, presently,
again. One, the younger, POD, *stirs and groans. He sits*
up and stares round at the audience.

POD: Good heavens . . . Mat.

　　　[MAT *doesn't stir.*]

I had the strangest dream. I was lying on a stretch of
sand somewhere. I opened my eyes and a woman had
hold of my feet and was pulling me into the sea. I
wonder what that means. I suppose it was a woman.
I've only seen pictures. My brother used to draw them
in the sand when he'd nothing better to do. Which was
most of the time. Sometimes with his finger, sometimes with his foot. He became very good at drawing
with his foot, he could rattle off a woman in no time at
all. The beach was covered with them. They went half-
way round the island. How good they were I can't say,
I'm no judge. They weren't very detailed. Perhaps
women aren't. And detail's difficult in dry sand unless
you draw big and that's difficult with your foot, unless
you hop backwards, and that jogs the outline; the result
isn't pleasing. He also tried sitting in a palm tree with a
long stick. He could draw very big that way, big
women. Only a stick that length is difficult to control.
The point tended to dig into the sand. Then he over-
stretched himself and fell out of the tree. Nearly broke
his neck. For the sake of art. Mind you, he's never seen a
woman either. Only pictures. Our father used to draw
them in the sand. He was drawing a woman in the sand
the day he died. With his finger. He was trying a new
technique; drawing under water. A shark got him.
Drew *him* under water. Last time he tried that trick. I
don't know why I'm telling you all this. My mother
was a woman. I don't remember her. I seem to recall a
softness, a roundness, a smell of milk, but it could be
imagination. When she bore my brother the family fled

to a deseserted isle, to escape the wrath of women; it wasn't done to have boys; or husbands for that matter. She'd found him in a cave in the mountains. Then, on our island, she bore me. It's said she took one look at me and died soon after. So there we lived, my father and his two sons, not doing too badly on fish, wild pigs and coconuts. Then the old man died, as I explained, of artistic experimentation. Soon after, we two lads made a rude raft and floated off to find something else in life but wild pigs and coconuts, not wanting to go mad in each other's company. The raft, being too rude, broke up in a storm, and we were carried hither and left insensible on an unknown shore, where we are now discovered. It's an unlikely tale. But I'm sticking to it. Mat.

MAT: What was she like?

POD: Are you conscious?

MAT: No.

POD: What was who like?

MAT: Oh, God, I hate you. [*He sits up.*] I so hate the sound of your voice.

POD: That's all right, Mat.

MAT: I'd like to drop you out of a tree. Or hold you under water till you drowned.

POD: I quite understand.

MAT: The *woman* in your *dream*! What was she like?

POD: Oh. Well, I'm no judge, am I?

MAT: Was she old, young, buxom, tall, fair, deliciously bashful, maddeningly provocative, did she make you feel glad all over?

POD: Not particularly. She was all right. About middling, I suppose.

MAT: I'd like to strangle you slowly.

POD: She wasn't much like your pictures.

[MAT *grabs his arm fiercely.*]

MAT: How? How?

POD: How what?

MAT: How did she differ!

POD: She was dressed for one thing.

MAT: Then how did you know she was a woman? Tell me, tell me!

POD: I don't know. You're hurting my arm.

> [MAT *at once lets go, puts his head in his hands and sobs with frustration.*]

It was only a dream. Anyway, your pictures are just out-lines. She was . . .

MAT: What?

POD: More.

MAT: Was she like my outlines?

POD: How do I know? She was dressed.

MAT: What a waste of a good dream.

POD: I do think you're a bit obsessive on the subject.

MAT: For years I've been trying to dream of a woman. All I get is mandala symbols.

POD: Why don't you try trying to dream of a mandala symbol? There's an odd bird on this island. Did you hear it?

> [MAT *speaks more or less to the audience.*]

MAT: Consider my predicament. Living in a world in which men have been outlawed, persecuted, hunted down like animals, drowned at birth like mutants, and still are as far as I know. Unless we're the last on earth, as we may well be. Brought up without sight, sound or feel — oh, God! — of the opposite sex, knowing the world is full of them. Water, water, everywhere, what was that old line? Race memory crying out within me, a hunger in every fibre of my being, incapable of assuagement . . .

POD: I don't get that.

MAT: Then why dream of them, you lascivious swine?

POD: I'm going to have a pee in the sea.

> [*He stands up and moves towards the audience. A rope is tied from his ankle to that of* MAT. *The rope pulls* MAT *onto his back.*]

We're tied up.

MAT: Of course we are, you idiot. I did it.

POD: So you did. When our rude raft was breaking up you tied our ankles so that I wouldn't swim the wrong way. It was very brotherly of you.

MAT: I wanted to be sure of something to eat in case there was nothing here.

POD: Oh. Well, you are the oldest.

MAT: I'm hungry now.

POD: Can I have my pee first?

MAT: No.

POD: I'll go and look for some food. Shall I?
> [*He starts to walk off away from the audience, and again pulls* MAT *over.*]

MAT: Untie the rope.

POD: Yes, Mat. Good thinking. [*He tries.*] 'It's a funny old world that we live in . . .' I wish I knew the rest of that poem. It's the only poem I know. 'It's a funny old world that we live in . . .'

MAT: Shut up and untie the rope or I'll eat you on the spot.
> [*He reaches inside his shirt for his knife.*]

POD: I can't, the water's got at the knots.

MAT: I've lost my knife!

POD: That's a pity.

MAT: It's a disaster. What's a man without his knife? Bloody knots, who tied this?

POD: We'd better go together, hadn't we?
> [MAT *gets up.*]

MAT: Can I make one request of you?

POD: What's that, Mat?

MAT: When we pass a tree, do you think you could go by on the same side I do.

POD: Why's that? Oh, I see. I'll try that.
> [*They begin to walk.* MAT *stops, pulling* POD *to a halt.*]
> What's the matter?

MAT: [*in a hoarse whisper*] Human footprints!

POD: They're ours, Mat.

MAT: These, you fool.

POD: Yes, I noticed them. What do you think they mean?

MAT: People have been here.

POD: Good thinking.

MAT: Watching us. Men? Or — Oh, God!

POD: I really do need a pee.

MAT: Well, there's nothing for it. We can't stay here. God, I'm hungry in every sense of the word. Oh, to eat a woman, to *eat* a *woman* . . . I wonder if they're armed. Well, we're men; we must take courage, go forward together, stand together, fight together. Perhaps we can surprise and overpower them. Wreak our will on them. Prove our superiority.

POD: We'll certainly surprise them.

[*They exit.*]

SCENE THREE

As Scene One. VI, JO *and* DEE *are discovered. They per-*
form the chorus in something of a classical manner.
KAY *should be with them, but has not yet returned.* KAY
enters, however, at some time during the chorus, and
takes it up as best she can, being a little behind the
others.

CHORUS: Is there no escaping from the past?
Can we never escape the stranglehold of our dead past?
Long since, and none too soon, we women threw off
our chains.
Why, then, now, are we taunted with relics of our long
bondage?
Through the wisdom of woman we found the light and
right path;
Why now do you remind us of our former crooked
ways?
What is the purpose of this nasty discovery?
Our past is dead; why will it not lie down?

DEE: Which is all very well, but it doesn't solve the problem.

KAY: I couldn't find Sue.

JO: Did you look?

VI: After all, there are only two of them.

DEE: Isn't that enough?

JO: Two too many.

DEE: Let's crystallise the situation. Down there on the beach
are two representatives of the most dangerous and
destructive creature the world has ever known. Right?

JO: Right.

DEE: Where they've come from, we don't know. What we do
know is that they are up to no good. Right?

VI: How do we know that?

JO: I think we can take that for granted.

DEE: In fact, we are at a crisis-point. Now, of course, there is
a simple and neat solution to the problem.

KAY: What's that?

DEE: The painless despatch of the two creatures while still in
a state of insensibility by, for instance, the insertion of a

knife between the shoulder-blades or the dropping of a
large rock or some such from a height onto the heads.
The corpses could then be consigned to the sea and we
could continue as before.

VI: We can't do that.

DEE: Right, we can't. Because we are not, unfortunately,
murderously inclined.

VI: Unfortunately?

DEE: And so, being blessed with none of the animal viciousness and brutality characteristic of man, there is
nothing we can do but await their will.

JO: I find that rather defeatist.

DEE: Have you another suggestion?

JO: Yes. Er . . . Rope.

DEE: Rope?

JO: Find some rope.

KAY: Rope?

JO: Rope, find some rope!

          [KAY *exits into the hut.*]

Now, where shall we put them when we've bound them
hand and foot and brought them back here? Dig a hole
in the ground?

DEE: They'll tunnel out. They're famous for tunnelling in
adversity.

JO: A cage, then, some sort of cage. You're good at basket-
work.

          [DEE *shakes her head.*]

Can't you be constructive?

DEE: Very well, I will. Let's suppose we put them in a cage.
What do we do then? Keep them here for the rest of their
lives, feeding them, standing guard over them? They
won't give up, you know, they won't accustom themselves to it like pet canaries. They'll have nothing to do,
day after day, but give their minds to the problem of
how to get out, how to win. While we feed them.
They'll use all their inventiveness, all their guile, all
their deceit. They'll watch us, size us up, wait for us to
grow careless, start to pity them. They'll work on us.
They'll play us, and we'll let them, till they draw music

from our hearts. 'More,' we'll say, 'More sweet music.'
And then one day ...

VI: I'm going to take the poor creatures some food!

    [*She takes up some fruit from the table and exits. Enter* KAY *with a short bit of string.*]

KAY: This is all I can find.

DEE: I'm going to have some breakfast. I don't propose to be ravished on an empty stomach.

JO: If we all tied our girdles together ...

DEE: I'm not parting with my girdle.

KAY: Don't you think we may be jumping to conclusions? I mean, after all, they may not be too bad. I mean they may be amenable.

DEE: To what?

KAY: If we were nice to them, I mean, they might be nice to us. I mean, it's a matter of communication. Isn't it? I feel perhaps I could communicate with them. I do feel that.

    [*A scream off.* DEE *and* JO *pick up a knife and fork each from the table.*]

There, you see, she's probably frightened them.

    [POD, MAT *and* VI *enter.* POD *and* MAT *are still roped together.* MAT *is holding* VI, *who holds the fruit.*]

MAT: Nobody's to move or she gets it!

    [*For a moment nobody does move.* DEE *and* JO *stand with their knives and forks at the ready.*]

KAY: [*not very convincingly*] Oh, horror ...

POD: Look, Mat, food.

MAT: Women, hundreds of women. And food.

    [*He begins to laugh maniacally, then controls himself.*]

Don't move! Drop your weapons!

    [KAY *steps forward.*]

KAY: Parlez-vous français?

MAT: Stop! What's she saying?

POD: Sounds like a foreign language, Mat.

KAY: Sprechen Sie Deutsch? Habla Español?

MAT: Keep back! Don't think you can fool me with your tricks.

VI: Do let go, I'm not going to hurt you.

MAT: Silence! I know your tricks with the poisoned food, I know them all. Keep back! One move and I'll, I'll —!
    [KAY *tries him with Italian and Russian.*]

POD: I don't think they understand you.

VI: He's terrified, poor creature. Stop pointing those knives at him.

POD: I still haven't had my pee, Mat.
    [KAY *tries him with Urdu and rather halting English.*]

MAT: Silence! [*His voice has risen to a high pitch.*]

KAY: I think he wants us to be quiet.

MAT: Silence!
    [*Silence.*]

POD: What do we do now —?

MAT: Silence!
    [*Silence. All look at* MAT, *since he has obviously decided to take control. He casts about him, realising his vulnerable position.*]
    Nobody move!
    [*Nobody does. He points to the food on the table.*]
    Bring me food and make it quick.
    [*Nobody moves.*]
    Do you hear me?

POD: They don't understand you, Mat.

MAT: I can see that!

POD: Why don't you eat what you've got?

MAT: It's poisoned, you fool. You think they'd bring food if it wasn't poisoned?

POD: Oh.

MAT: Get me some.

POD: From over there?

MAT: Yes.

POD: Right.
    [*He clears his throat and begins to stroll nonchalantly toward the table.*]
    I'm just going to get some of that, not to worry ...
    [*The rope brings him up short, nearly having* MAT *over.*]

MAT: Nobody move!
                    [POD *stops with one leg in the air.*]
           Put your leg down, you idiot. Take her knife.
                    [*The* WOMEN *by now have, after this display,
                    somewhat lost their fear, and have lowered
                    their points.*]
POD: Hers?
MAT: Yes.
POD: Her knife.
MAT: Yes, her knife.
POD: Right.
                    [MAT *carefully edges forward with* VI *to give*
                    POD *enough rope to advance.*]
           Do you think I might have your knife? Your . . .
                    [*He makes sawing actions.*]
MAT: Give him the knife or she gets it. *Give — him — knife
           — or she — gets it.*
                    [*He gestures to make himself understood.*]
POD: I don't think she's with you.
                    [KAY *tries him with Hebrew.*]
MAT: Silence!
                    [*The penny drops for* JO.]
JO: Oh, *silence.*
MAT: Silence!
JO: Silence.
MAT: Silence!
JO: [*to the others*] Do you see? Silence!
MAT: Silence or she gets it!
JO: [*delighted*] Silence!
MAT: Take the knife.
POD: Take it.
MAT: Yes.
POD: Right. Excuse me . . . Might I have your knife?
                    [*But as he reaches for it* DEE *raises her knife
                    again and retreats.* POD *follows cautiously,
                    with* MAT *and* VI *shuffling behind. They reach
                    the table.*]
MAT: Stop!
                    [POD *stops.*]
JO: Stop. Do you see? He means stop.

MAT: Silence!
JO: We'll soon pick up the language.
            [KAY *tries him with Swahili.*]
MAT: Silence!
POD: What do we do now, Mat?
MAT: Nothing. We've reached a point of advantage.
POD: Have we?
MAT: We've captured their supplies. They've been forced to
            withdraw. They know who's master now. We'll eat and
            consider our position.
POD: Right.
            [*They eat.*]
KAY: Oh, and they're hungry, look.
JO: Ah . . .
            [MAT *attempts a 'Silence!' with his mouth full,
            then gives up.*]
POD: Honey, Mat. I've never had honey before. There wasn't
            any on our old island.
            [MAT *mumbles something.*]
            What's that?
MAT: I said, then how do you know it's honey?
POD: That's a point.
DEE: Honey.
            [*She points to the honey.* POD *looks up.*]
POD: What?
DEE: Honey.
POD: Oh. Yes. *Honey.*
DEE: Honey.
POD: Honey.
MAT: Keep back or she gets it!
            [DEE *jumps back at his voice.*]
            Eat your food.
POD: Honey.
            [*He gives the thumbs-up sign to* DEE.]
            Seem quite friendly, don't they, Mat?
MAT: They're gulling us. Lulling us.
POD: Do you think so?
MAT: They don't fool me. You perhaps; you'll be the first to
            go. What a relief that'll be.
POD: Yes, but Mat —

MAT: Eat your food. We'll need all our strength.

POD: What for?

MAT: To wreak our will.

DEE: They don't *look* very vicious.

JO: Don't be taken in by that. Remember what they've done
      through history.

KAY: Yes, but not these.

DEE: Is he hurting you?

VI: No, actually. Not much. He's frightened, poor soul.
      That's why he's gripping so tight.

KAY: Reassure him. Communicate with him.

VI: I'm doing perfectly well, thank you. I don't think you
      could do any better.

KAY: You're joking. [*She advances to the table.*] Would you
      like some coconut milk?

MAT: Back! Back!

VI: Get away, you're disturbing him.

KAY: Nonsense. Here you are, my good man. I shan't harm
      you. [*She offers him some coconut milk.*] Here, drink
      it.
                  [*He makes a sudden grab and holds her wrist.*]

MAT: Ah! Now! Got you! Don't think you can gull me!

KAY: Ooh . . .

VI: Now you've made him angry.

JO: So much for communication.

KAY: What a strong grip he has.

MAT: Ah. Now then.

POD: What are you going to do now, Mat?

MAT: What?

POD: Do you want me to feed you?

MAT: That's two of them taken prisoner. [*He looks round for
      the next thing to do.*] We need some rope to tie them up.

POD: Shall I go look for some?
                  [*He begins to go, forgetting the ankle rope.*]

MAT: No! That. Round her waist. Untie it.

POD: Me?

MAT: Quick.

POD: Right. Do you think I might . . .

KAY: Oh horror, what are you doing? No, just pull that one.

POD: I've got it, Mat.

MAT: Tie her wrist.

POD: Right.

VI: You see what you've done now?

KAY: Yes.

MAT: Now my wrist.

POD: Good thinking, Mat. Then she'll have you prisoner.

MAT: I'll have *her* prisoner.

POD: Ah.

MAT: Now the other one.

POD: Other what?

MAT: Waist. Rope. Woman.

POD: Oh. Yes. You know, I think a pattern's emerging from all this.

[*He takes* VI's *girdle.*]

VI: Just what do you think you're doing?

JO: Don't struggle.

VI: But he's —

JO: Let him have it.

POD: Here you are, Mat. Tie her wrist?

MAT: Yes.

POD: Right. You see, I pick things up quite quickly if you give me time. We'll have it all shipshape before we know where we are. 'It's a funny old world that we live in, Da da dadada dadada . . .'

JO: I think the time has come to go outside our normal natures. We must forget for a moment that we are the soul of gentleness with any form of violence anathema to us. We must for a moment behave as men.

DEE: What have you got in mind?

JO: Just do as I say?

MAT: What's she saying?

POD: I don't know, Mat. Where do I tie the other end?

DEE: He can't be such a fool as to tie it to —

MAT: Tie it to your wrist, you fool.

POD: I don't think I can do that.

MAT: Come here, I'll do it. Back! Back!

DEE: He is.

MAT: Silence!

POD: When am I going to be able to make water, Mat?

MAT: In a moment. We shall take them off with us, prisoners, hostages, to wreak our will on them.

POD: How do we do that?

MAT: Fill your shirt with food and shut up.

POD: But I'm wearing it.

> [MAT *begins to put food down his shirt front.*]

Oh. Right.

> [*He does the same.*]

KAY: I think they're preparing for a journey.

JO: Now listen, you two; when I give the word, you are to pull on your girdles as hard as you can. Understood?

KAY: What for?

JO: Just do it. Dee — stand ready.

DEE: For what?

JO: To pounce.

DEE: You're joking.

VI: Don't you think you're being rather uncharacteristic? No good will come of it, you know.

JO: Ready . . .

DEE: I think you're making a big mistake.

JO: Pull!

> [KAY *pulls, walking away from* MAT. MAT *follows.*]

MAT: Stop! Silence!

> [*His ankle rope brings him up short. He goes over.* VI *watches this with interest, then with a little tug of her girdle she has* POD *over.* JO *leaps to where they are lying, brandishing her knife and fork.*]

JO: Victory! On them!

> [DEE *stands where she was, shaking her head.*]

MAT: Treacherous bitches!

JO: Oh, what's the use . . .?

> [POD *starts to get up. With a casual flick of the wrist,* VI *has him over again.*]

POD: Looks like another stalemate.

MAT: Oh, I hate you. I wish she'd stick her knife in your guts. I want to lie here and see it happen before she does for me.

DEE: Well, what do you do now?
POD: Mat ...
MAT: What?
POD: If I don't go soon I shall do it in my trousers.

SCENE FOUR

A jungle glade. Exotic bird calls are heard. SUE *enters, carrying flowers.*

SUE: How sweet life is. Here on this island we want for nothing. The clime is clement, and food to our liking always within reach. The woods are full of creatures, but they are not hurtful, having nor sting nor bite; creatures here do not prey on one another, and therefore do not know fear, having only that proper sense of caution necessary, for example, to prevent the lesser of them being trod upon by the greater. You may see them in the undergrowth, watching me with gentle curiosity — if your eyes are sharp enough.

     [She sighs.]

And yet, ever and again, I sigh. Strange. I am completely happy. Let me sit for a while on this convenient hummock and dwell a little on sighs, and dreams, and happiness, though not to get boring with it.

     [She sits with her flowers.]

The fact is . . . Here's a pretty one . . . When we first came here, I was happy without knowing it. Or rather, without knowing I knew it . . . At least, the question never arose. Perhaps I knew that I knew it without knowing I knew . . . A kind of orchid this, with a strange yearning smell as of the linden when the sap falls . . . I ate when I was hungry, swam in the sea, lay in the sun, laughed with my sisters . . . I never thought, shall I eat, shall I swim? I did it, that was all and enough . . . I've lately taken to picking so many flowers on every possible occasion . . . Not that it matters, there are flowers and to spare, the blessed things grow overnight . . . This lacks a petal.

     [She throws one away.]

I came upon two creatures one day mating in the woods, in the way creatures do and as humankind did in the old days, before it became mercifully unnecessary. I watched them for a while and then a kind of sad-

ness took me and I turned away . . . I filled the house
with flowers that day . . . They seemed not to like what
they did . . . And yet they did it . . . As is the way with
lesser creatures, having no reason, only instinct . . . So
we were once . . . But as I am aware of my happiness, so
perhaps are they unaware of their discomfort . . . As it
must surely be . . . It seems obvious to me that everything that is, must be good. How could it be, otherwise? Therefore to want what is not is a useless exer-
cise. And yet, in the middle of happiness I say to myself:
'I am completely happy', and hearing my words I
think: 'How do I know what complete happiness is, or
if this is it, or if there is something more?' This is
getting me nowhere . . . But of course there's nowhere I
need get . . . I'll pick some more flowers. I'm sorry to
have troubled you.

> [*She begins to leave. There is the sound of
> voices approaching. The voices are of* MAT *and*
> POD *but the words are in an unknown tongue.*]

What can that be? Human voices; but on a low note,
and speaking an unknown tongue. [*She listens.*] All
that is, is good; therefore there's nothing can harm me.
Even so, I'll do as the wood creatures and watch with
caution.

> [*She conceals herself.* MAT, POD *and* KAY *enter,
> tied as before.* MAT *comes on first, with* KAY
> *close behind. As* POD *appears he is jerked to a
> standstill by* VI *who has dawdled offstage. This
> communicates itself through* MAT *to* KAY, *who
> seems quite content with her lot .* MAT *falls.*]

KAY: Oh, I'm so sorry.
MAT: [*to* POD] Idiot! Why can't you keep up?
POD: Sorry, Mat, it's her. She keeps hanging back.
MAT: Bloody shambles . . . Ah! [*He holds his ankle.*]
KAY: Let me help you.
> [*She makes to do so.*]
MAT: Back!
KAY: I'm not going to hurt you.
> [*But she keeps her distance all the same.*]

MAT: Did you see that? Turned on me, the bitch.
[VI *enters.*]

KAY: Do keep up, Vi; it makes things so difficult for the rest of us.

MAT: Silence! I've sprained my bloody ankle now.

KAY: Look, he's hurt his ankle.

MAT: We'll rest.

POD: I could do with a rest.

KAY: I think we're having a rest.
[*She sits down.*]

MAT: What's she saying?

POD: I don't know, Mat.

MAT: Probably plotting something. Watch every move, don't take your eyes off them.
[*He takes some fruit out of his shirt and eats it moodily. There is a pause as they all take their ease.*]

POD: 'It's a funny old . . .' Mat.

MAT: What?

POD: Do you ever get the feeling you've been here before?

MAT: You said that ten minutes ago. You're boring enough without repeating yourself.

POD: Yes, Mat. It was just that tree reminded me of it. That one there with the funny shape. You remember.
[MAT *looks at him, then at the tree.*]

MAT: Oh God . . .

POD: Do you remember, I pointed out that tree and said, 'Do you ever get that feeling you've been here before?' and it turned out we had been? That's what reminded me, seeing that tree again. Funny the way one remembers things.

MAT: We've come round in a circle again.

POD: I thought perhaps we had.

MAT: Shut up and let me think.

POD: Yes, Mat.
[*He speaks more or less to the audience.*]
I suppose it's of the nature of things that nothing ever lasts forever, or anywhere near it. Everything alters, life is a constant changing from one stalemate to the next.

Whatever happens you can therefore say to yourself: it can only happen for just so long, and then it'll change to something else which might go on even longer. On an island one has time for philosophy, though it's as useless there as anywhere else. And so, instead of lying forever between two women while a third woman stood over us with a knife and fork, the scene has changed; we've reached a further plateau. As to how, the details are irrelevant, I won't bore you with them. Well, I will. We realised after a time, that is to say Mat realised, that the woman with the knife and fork had no intention of using them. There was a kind of hesitancy, a draw-ing back, as if she would rather not have been put in a position which demanded, if it were to have any validity as an offensive gesture, the readiness to carve a slice or two if necessary off the enemy — as I suppose she quite rightly considered us. In short, her posture lacked conviction. And so, after ten or twenty minutes, we began to edge away on our arses and elbows. She edged after us, still wielding the knife and fork as if we were a not too appetising meal on wheels; and looking so unhappy with it that we decided on a counter-attack and edged once more forward. That is to say, Mat did, and I was forced to follow suit. She edged away. This toing and froing went on for some time until Mat decided on a strategic retreat with our booty. The booty co-operated, or at least put up no great resistance. The other women followed, at a safe distance, brandishing their cutlery, and then, after talking among them-selves, left us. Mat assumes they've gone off to plan a counter-attack at night; and after working themselves into a frenzy of bloodlust by dancing naked in the setting sun they'll butcher us unmercifully and throw our corpses into the sea, keeping only our male members tied to their girdles as trophies. It seems to me unlikely, but everything's both possible and un-important. If I'm to be thrown butchered into the sea I don't much care what I take with me and what I leave behind. Another possibility, which seems to me more

likely, is that we've hit some kind of loop or snag in our
personal history; that we'll continue to circle back to
this place, as we have twice already, until the end of
time, and that this spot will echo forever with the
recurrent phrase: do you ever get that feeling you've
been here before? It would seem to me to reconcile
nicely the two main chacteristics of life, the constant
change and the never getting anywhere. But there I go
philosophising again. It's a strange island, that's for
sure, and not unmindful of our presence, I think. A
sprained ankle? Such things don't happen so
conveniently — not outside fiction. Which, of course, I
suppose this may well be. In which case —

MAT: I've got it! The perfect solution. Brilliant. All we've got
to do is —. No, that won't do.

         [*He returns to his cogitations.*]

VI: I'm beginning to entertain doubts as to the efficiency of
these two.

KAY: We have to assume they know what they're doing.

VI: Why?

KAY: I don't know.

VI: There are two possibilities. The plan they have in hand
is so devilishly ingenious it's beyond the wit of women;
or they're a couple of idiots.

KAY: The world couldn't have been run by idiots, surely.
Perhaps it's the way of men, that they walk in circles
tied together.

VI: Has it occurred to you that all we know about men is
what we've been told, at third or fourth hand?

KAY: I *was* expecting something more definite. An early
ravishment. I'd quite steeled myself to it. I won't go so
far as to say I feel a sense of slight . . .

MAT: Silence!

VI: Be quiet, do. Even when I was very young I took what I
was told about men with a certain reserve, more as
myth than as history. Not that I ever doubted they were
dangerously vicious and nasty, the facts of history
showed that. What I resisted was the idea that they were
naturally so. I couldn't believe nature to be so illogical
as to produce a creature whose destiny was to tear the

world to pieces and himself with it. So, I thought, the viciousness must have been implanted or picked up by accident on the way; it was an unnatural growth and so removable. I even wondered whether woman was partly responsible for not curing the ailment less crudely than by killing the patient. This is why I took food to these two and went along with them. But maybe I was wrong. Perhaps they're not real men. They seem more stupid than brutal, though there's not much in it. I haven't even felt any of the fabled fatal charm which the old tales tell us could lure a woman to degradation and doom.

KAY: Haven't you?

VI: Have you?

KAY: There is a kind of macabre fascination.

VI: You always were suggestible. Anyway, I'm going no further without some sign of logical behaviour.

POD: Mat . . .

MAT: Why the devil aren't you thinking? Why leave it all to me?

POD: You know I'm no good at it.

MAT: Oh, I loathe you. I wish I'd left you to swim the wrong way.

POD: Mat, don't you think it would be a good idea to get rid of those two?

MAT: What, eat them?

POD: I was thinking more on the lines of let them go.

MAT: Our hostages? Our prisoners? Are you mad? Our bargaining counter? Our only asset? Our women?

POD: Well, this one anyway.

MAT: But she's yours!

POD: But I don't want her, Mat. I don't know what to do with her.

MAT: You *are* mad.

POD: She's got a way of looking at me makes me feel silly.

MAT: Ha!

POD: Every time I catch her looking at me I either trip over my own feet or walk into a tree. As for taking a pee . . . It took all the joy out of it.

MAT: Help me up.

POD: What?

MAT: We're going on. Help me up.

POD: We'll only go round in a circle again. Couldn't we just sit here and wait till we'd have arrived?

MAT: Help me up. I've sprained my ankle.

KAY: He's hurt his ankle, he wants helping up.

MAT: Silence.

VI: Nothing much up top, I'm convinced of it. A mindless brute, I'm afraid.

MAT: Silence.

VI: Do stop saying that.

MAT: Help me up.

KAY: I'll help him up.

MAT: Back!

> [*He cries out in pain.*]

POD: [*to* KAY] He's sprained his ankle.

KAY: What?

> [POD *points to his own ankle and grimaces.*]

POD: Ankle. Aaah. Hurt it. Ooh . . .

VI: He's hurt *his* ankle.

MAT: Help me up.

POD: Right, Mat.

> [*He tries to get up to help* MAT *but because of* VI's *girdle he can't make it.*]

KAY: Help him up.

VI: I'm not moving till I see a glimmer of human intelligence.

POD: Excuse me . . .

MAT: What are you waiting for? Help me up.

POD: I can't, Mat. She won't let me up.

MAT: Oh, good God . . .

> [POD *pulls on his girdle.*]

POD: Let me *up.*

VI: Don't *do* that.

> [*She tugs back.* POD, *caught off balance half up and half down, falls, tugging on* MAT's *foot.* MAT *cries out in pain.* POD *cries out in pain.*]

POD: I think I've sprained my ankle.

KAY: Aah . . . let me massage your ankle.

MAT: Back!

VI: It's no use trying to help them, they obviously don't understand such things.

MAT: Si — !

VI: Stop that, do, or I shall get angry.

POD: Mat . . .

[*Long pause.*]

MAT: Hit her.

POD: What?

MAT: Fetch her one. Lay about her. Show her who's master!

POD: I don't know who's master! I'm sick of this! As far as I can see, if I'm tied up to someone I'm just as much their prisoner as they are my prisoner!

[MAT *stares, surprised at his outburst.*]

Sorry, Mat. Almost lost my temper there.

[*Pause.*]

MAT: I need a pee.

POD: [*mumbles*] Now you know what it's like . . .

MAT: What?

POD: Nothing?

MAT: What a pitiful creature you are, what a spineless . . . A man? You're not a man.

POD: No, Mat.

[*Pause.*]

MAT: There's something about this place. Here am I, a member of the master-race, renowned for its ingenuity, audacity, perspicacity, and so on. Ruthless in its pursuit of the twin goals of personal aggrandisement and the bringing of order into an untidy world for the greater good and if necessary by force. Taming, conquering and always winning out in the end. So what am I doing tied like a bead on a string with a sprained ankle and a shirt full of fruit? What the devil is going on!

POD: I don't know, Mat —

MAT: Shut up!

POD: Sorry —

MAT: Shut up!

POD: Yes, Mat —

MAT: Shut up! I want silence. I'm sick of it.

> [*Silence. Then the conch is heard, a single long note.*]

Silence!

> [*At the same time there is a second note, but cut short apparently by his cry. A pause.*]

'As the two men strode into the clearing, the women cowered back in fear, overawed by the sight of these superior beings. "We are your masters" said the elder of the two, whose manner and bearing marked him out as a natural leader. "Remember that and you won't get hurt." Seizing one of the women, he dragged her into the rude hut. At first she resisted, fighting and tearing like a wild thing; but to no avail. Then, softening, she clung to him imploringly as he wreaked his will. On her. "More," she murmured, "More. My master." Meanwhile the others had prepared a sumptuous banquet of roast pig, baked fish and all manner of exotic jungle dishes and stood ready to do the bidding of these godlike creatures, accepting gladly their natural supremacy ...' I want to go back to the beginning again ...

VI: Kay ...

KAY: Hm?

VI: I've got an idea. Listen, if you crawled round there — and I crawled round there ...

KAY: Then we'd ...

VI: Yes.

KAY: And then what?

VI: We can work that out when we've done it.

KAY: Can't we let events take their course?

VI: They will be, won't they?

KAY: All right, then. We'll give it a whirl.

VI: Right. Off we go.

> [VI *crawls quickly round one way.* KAY *crawls quickly round the other.*]

MAT: Silence. Back.

VI: Pull.

> [*They pull.* MAT *and* POD *find themselves pulled together and encircled by the girdles.*]

MAT: Let me out!
[*He manages to catch hold of* KAY's *free wrist.*]

KAY: Ooh ...

VI: Let go of her!
[VI *tries to free* KAY's *wrist. They are now hopelessly entangled. They struggle for a while, then give up.*]

MAT: Bitches!

POD: Looks like another stalemate, Mat.

KAY: If there is a next step, I can't think what it is.
[*Pause.*]

MAT: And yet, you know, it's a strange thing, that underneath it all, even while I rant and roar and struggle for supremacy, power and the satisfaction of my desires, which are after all the only real things in life, even while I do all that there's an odd uneasy feeling that it's all a kind of game, a kind of play-acting, that someone ... It's this bloody island! A strange lassitude, a sort of melting, a letting go, a kind of acceptance; as if I'm not really in control, as if it has all been played out before, long ago; as if it really doesn't matter after all ...

POD: I know what you mean, Mat.

MAT: What's that noise?
[*The breeze has begun to rise in the treetops; a strange, sweet, sighing music makes itself heard.*]

POD: Sounds like music.

VI: It's the music.

KAY: Here we go.

VI: What did we do that for?

KAY: I don't know.

VI: Helpless. Like children, like lost children, children lost in a wood, children far from home ...

KAY: They need, they need ...

MAT: [*feebly*] Silence ... Back ...

KAY: They need, they need ...
[*She touches him.*]

MAT: Oh ...

KAY: Ooh ...

VI: Gentle like children, vulnerable like children,

waking in a wood, not knowing how we came there,
not knowing where it began or how it will end or what
is to become of us . . .

POD: Mat . . .

MAT: Hm?

POD: Do you remember our mother?

MAT: No . . . Yes . . .

> [KAY *smiles at him. He touches her. She touches
> him.*]

A gentle, a loving, a . . . No, I won't have it . . . A fondle,
a cradle, a letting, a letting . . .

KAY: A touching, a finding, a having, a giving, a . . . Have
me, let me have you, let us have one another . . .

POD: All I can imagine is a softness, a not having to . . . Good
heavens . . .

> [*Enter* SUE. *She comes up to him and gives him
> a flower. They gaze at one another.*]

SUE: Oh, brave new world . . .

SCENE FIVE

As Scene One. DEE *and* JO. JO *is blowing a blast on the conch. As she begins a second blast* DEE *breaks in.*

DEE: Do stop that.

JO: I thought we'd let them know we were thinking of them.

DEE: Who needs thinking about when they're where the action is? They're not thinking about us, that's for sure.

JO: It's a question of solidarity, isn't it?

DEE: A question of what?

JO: The way you talk anyone would think you envy them.

DEE: Envy them? Don't be ridiculous! You imagine I want to traipse over the countryside with those creatures? It's ludicrous. How dare you!

JO: All right!

DEE: They have a smell, did you notice, a peculiar smell.

JO: Mm.

DEE: I wonder if we smell to them.

[*Pause.*]

It is interesting, though, how as soon as a couple of men come on the scene, the action begins to centre on them. The fact that it was our island in the first place makes no difference. And that we're five to their two. Of course, being in a minority gives the advantage of scarcity value. But I'll bet if they were five and we were two it wouldn't make any difference. The fact is, they attract interest as rotten meat attracts flies. And what's left for us? We're stuck at home with nothing to do but domestic chores; and of course to talk about them. It's the old story. You see, I'm doing it now, talking about them, keeping interest alive till they deign to put in an appearance.

JO: Don't then. Let's talk about something else.

DEE: The washing up?

JO: The role of women in a changing society. The way I see it is this —

DEE: They get the dramatic action, what do we get? A lacuna.

JO: Don't keep on about it then. What's a lacuna?

DEE: A hole with nothing to fill it.

JO: I know the feeling. *Shall* we do the washing up? Take half each, have a race?

DEE: There you go.

JO: What do you mean?

DEE: Talking about races already; competitiveness. We're not competitive people, we're past all that. So why suggest it?

JO: I only —

DEE: I'll tell you: it's their influence. It's happening already. They're unsettling us; corrupting us.

JO: We should have stayed on their heels; waited for a favourable opportunity.

DEE: To do what?

JO: I don't know!

DEE: Follow them around in ever-decreasing circles? Thank you, no, I've better things to do.

JO: Only you haven't, have you?

DEE: Stuck here like a spare prick at a wedding . . . Whatever that means . . .

JO: I don't know what you're so upset about. They haven't done anything to you. You can carry on doing whatever you usually do.

DEE: Of course I can't!

JO: Why not!

DEE: Because they're *here*! That's just it. They exert a kind of influence; an atmosphere. Action at a distance. They take over. They get inside our heads. The buggers. Quite true, I'm free to carry on just as before, do what I usually do, or not do what I usually don't do. Only suddenly I start to *question* what I'm doing, think: what am I doing, am I enjoying it, should I be doing something else, what am I here for? We used to just do the washing up and be done with it; now you suggest having a race with it, and I think, bugger the washing up. They've corrupted us already. Well, I don't want to talk about them.

[*Pause.*]

They're not really what I imagined, you know.

JO: I thought you didn't want to talk about them.

DEE: Why shouldn't I talk about them? I'm not so obsessed with them I have to not talk about them, believe me.

JO: What?

DEE: But I won't if it upsets you.

JO: Go ahead.

DEE: I imagined something a little more, how shall I say? Impressive. Somewhat terrifying and brutish.

JO: Be fair, they are brutish.

DEE: Well, they're not what I had in mind.

JO: I don't think I had anything in mind.

DEE: Well neither did I, of course.

JO: I know what you mean, though. If I had been expecting anything, they'd be a disappointment.

DEE: It's rather difficult to credit them with all the damage their race is supposed to have done.

JO: Supposed to?

DEE: *Has* done. Though I see now their influence is more insidious than direct. They get at our minds, make us dissatisfied, competitive. Like you wanting to turn a perfectly normal domestic operation into a race.

JO: Do shut up about that.

DEE: As for direct action, those two would make heavy weather of destroying a blancmange.

JO: They're certainly stupid. I think we should have killed them when we had the chance.

DEE: I don't know . . .

JO: If they're so insidious —

DEE: If we keep our wits about us. After all, we don't want to play their game. Violence. Playing into their hands. Right into their hands . . . What's a blancmange?

JO: I don't know.

DEE: Anyway, they don't come up to expectation.

JO: And a good thing too.

DEE: That goes without saying.

JO: We'll say it all the same.

DEE: If they did we'd be done for by now.

JO: So thank God for incompetence.

DEE: Absolutely.
      [*Pause.*]
JO: If who did what?
DEE: What?
JO: You said if they did.
DEE: Did I?
JO: Did you, what?
DEE: Hm?
      [*Pause.* JO *suddenly shakes her head violently.*]
JO: That bloody breeze is coming up again.
DEE: Is that what it is?
JO: Look, the treetops are beginning to move.
DEE: No music yet.
JO: It won't be long. It always starts like this. Subliminal. I wonder if they'll be affected by it.
DEE: Who?
JO: Pull yourself together. Them.
DEE: I don't suppose so. The coarse-grained. No minds, just bodies. But if they're not and we are they'll have a ball.
JO: If they are and we are they'll have a ball. Well, here we go.
DEE: Off on a trip to never-never land.
JO: Out of one unreality into another. I never know whether to look forward to it or not.
DEE: Why not?
JO: It seems like a kind of opting out.
DEE: We don't opt it. It opts us.
      [*Pause.*]
JO: The transition is always a little disconcerting. Not knowing if you're gliding out of a dream or into one, or slipping perhaps from one dream into another. Difficult enough at the best of times on this island, where you're never quite sure where reality stops and imagination takes over; or even whether it's not all imaginary, the whole of our experience a conjuring up from elsewhere; it's certainly possible, or certainly can't be disproved, that we and our world are no more than a passing fancy in a mind which has nothing

better to do than dream us up; so that when that mind sleeps or tires of us, goes off you might say for a cup of coffee, there comes a kind of abeyance into our lives, an interval of which we know nothing.

[*The music comes up.*]

We say life seems to be real; but what would be the difference if it seemed to be imaginary . . .? We certainly take it on trust . . . Not that it matters whether we do or not . . .

DEE: You're philosophising; those bloody men again . . . [*She says this without rancour.*]

JO: On the other hand . . .

DEE: Of what!

JO: On the other hand, God works in a mysterious way. Her wonders to perform.

DEE: You can say that again.

JO: After all, we are faced with a *fait accompli.* One doesn't want to take a negative attitude to life.

DEE: Do you mean you've changed your mind about the advisability of killing them?

JO: All I'm saying is, one needs to be careful about negating experience. One needs to think twice, that's all I'm saying.

DEE: I do absolutely agree. I suppose you could hold that any experience is good — within reason.

JO: Not that I've been un — dissatisfied; this island provides all our needs, all our basic needs.

DEE: Leaving aside any needs we may know nothing of and therefore not know we need them.

JO: Exactly. But after all, one has to allow oneself to . . .

DEE: Grow.

JO: To grow; which doesn't mean scrabbling about for new sensations like a pig after truffles —

DEE: What are truffles?

JO: But neither perhaps should we bury our heads in the sand like, like . . .

DEE: It would show a distrust for . . .

JO: Life, yes, which has seemed to be on our side until now, or at least neutral.

DEE: There is something to be said for saying 'yes' to life.

JO: Or at any rate 'perhaps'. And then there's the question of, how shall I put it, the complementarity of it. The yin and the yang of it.

DEE: You think we've erred rather on the yin side?

JO: One should embrace life, I suppose, in all its . . .

DEE: Let's go and find them.

JO: Let's do that. Without prejudice.

DEE: Who knows, perhaps we can come to a *modus vivendi*.

JO: A *modus vivendi* with a *fait accompli*.

DEE: Listen. Someone's coming.

> [*They stop, on their way out.* VI *enters, her girdle dangling from her wrist.*]

JO: What are you doing here?

VI: I was *de trop*.

DEE: You were what?

VI: Sue arrived. With a flower. The young man untied me; and she tied herself. Then they began to do as the woodland creatures do. I watched for a while, but seemed not to be needed. I brought their fruit, it was getting in the way.

JO: With their ankles still tied together?

VI: It didn't seem to bother them.

> [JO *and* DEE *begin to leave.*]

I wouldn't go if I were you. It's rather an exclusive activity.

SCENE SIX

As Scene Four. MAT *and* POD *lie asleep, still tied by the ankles.* SUE *sleeps alongside* POD. *But* KAY *is awake, sitting up.*

KAY: What a very unusual experience. Not at all unpleasant. I could easily imagine it developing into a habit. Would I mind that? [*She considers* MAT *for a moment.*] I don't think I would. Though I do see a danger. We've grown used to self-sufficiency on this island; we're dependent on no-one. Everything we want is available on the moment, or has been. The trees, for example, put forth their fruit anew as fast as we pluck it, and as if by magic, so that the desire for food and its assuagement are as it were the same; one is, while hungry, satisfied, and then hungry no more. With this strange new fruit, on the other hand, the desire seems to increase with the eating — at least up to a point which I have so far not been allowed to reach. And there is but the one tree, whose magic seems after a while a little on the slow side; so that, reaching out one's hand once more to the branch, one encounters at last only — I won't labour the point.

[*She shakes* MAT *gently.*]

Hello.

[MAT *grunts in his sleep.*]

You see? This raises a question: if eating a new delicious fruit does nothing but leave you hungrier than before you started, is it perhaps better to leave the fruit alone? And what about the others? I foresee certain difficulties if they get a taste for it ... Wake up!

[MAT *grunts again and turns away from her.*]

Of course there's always the other one. He seemed to have more of a lasting quality, more of duration ... from what I could gather ...

[*She leans across* MAT *and shakes* POD.]

Excuse me ...

SUE: Take your hands off my man, you bitch, or I'll claw your eyes out!

[*She sits up.*]

KAY: I beg your pardon, I'm sure.

SUE: Oh, my own, my love, my own, own, own love! Make me yours, keep me yours, own me!

[*She embraces* POD]

KAY: Are you mad? What are you saying?

SUE: I want to sacrifice myself to you. Hurt me, I want you to destroy me.

KAY: Sue, behave yourself.

SUE: Keep away, you're not touching him, he's mine.

KAY: How can a person be yours?

SUE: I don't know, but he is. [*to the audience*] A revelation it was; like the sudden opening of a new pair of eyes onto a new world all of delight. Nothing was separate, nothing beyond reach, nothing forbidden; to want was to have, to take was to give, there was no past, no future; I was what I saw, became what I touched, we were the world, we were each other, we burned forever and were forever whole and entire to burn again, there was only the burning ...

KAY: What a vivid imagination you have.

SUE: It wasn't imagination, it happened.

KAY: Well, it wasn't my experience.

SUE: Of course it wasn't. No-one has what we have, no-one has ever done what we do. We live in a private world of pure magic never before discovered.

KAY: I think we'd better have a talk about this. Untie your wrist.

[KAY *begins to untie her wrist.*]

SUE: Take me away, my love, my own. I hate the world, I hate other people, they don't exist, there's only us. All the rest —

KAY: Oh, do be quiet! Untie your wrist.

SUE: What for?

KAY: This needs discussing. The experience doesn't seem to have done you much good.

SUE: There's nothing to discuss. I'm his forever, he's mine forever —

KAY: Shut up and untie your wrist.

SUE: I won't leave him.

KAY: You can come back.

SUE: He may not be here.

KAY: Then let him find you. It'll prove to you how much he wants you.

SUE: That's true. What a good idea.

KAY: I've heard of this kind of thing . . .

SUE: What kind of thing?

KAY: Never mind. Give me the end. Quick, before they wake up.

> [KAY *takes the two girdle ends. She ties* POD's *right wrist to* MAT's *right wrist, the girdle passing behind* MAT's *back; and* MAT's *left wrist to* POD's *left wrist, the girdle passing behind* POD's *back.*]

There. That'll give them something to think about. [*She stands up.*] Come on.

SUE: Oh, my love — !

KAY: Come *on*.

> [*She takes* SUE *off-stage. Pause.* POD *stirs and wakes.*]

POD: Good heavens . . . What a dream, eh . . .? Extraordinary . . . Is *that* what Mat was trying to dream about, all those years? Bit of a revelation, really. All right it was. A taste of heaven, a foretaste of eternity. The earth disappeared, the skies parted, and I was up there, wandering among the stars, up, up, up . . . I wouldn't mind some more of that . . . I need a pee.

> [*He goes to get up and discovers his bonds.*]

Hello, it's got worse. Mat . . .

> [*He pulls on his right wrist.* MAT *grunts. He pulls on his left wrist.*]

Did we swim ashore like this? Mat . . .

> [MAT *gives a groan, sits up and looks at* POD.]

MAT: Oh God, it's still you.

POD: Who did you expect? I had the most extraordinary dream, Mat. Did you?

MAT: Mind your own business.

POD: Mandala symbols again?

MAT: Crawling through the bloody things now.

POD: Hard luck. You won't believe this, but I dreamt about that thing you try to dream about. Most unlikely it was. There was this —

MAT: Wait a minute ... My God. Oh, my God. Where are they?

POD: There's only us, Mat.

MAT: I can see that. Where are they?

POD: Who?

MAT: The women!

POD: No. Mat, that was my dream. You're getting mixed up.

MAT: It wasn't a dream, you idiot!

POD: You mean it was — ? Good heavens. Do people *really* do that?

[MAT *discovers his bonds.*]

MAT: What's this?

POD: We seem to have got a bit more tied up.

MAT: Oh, the bitches. Oh, my God, the bitches ...

POD: That's not very nice, Mat, after what they did for us.

MAT: Did for us, what did for us?

POD: Well, it was all right, wasn't it?

MAT: Is *this* all right? Deceitful bitches.

POD: I mean before, you know. You did it too; I remember ... Well, part of the time ... Anyway, you were having a shot at it.

MAT: What are you getting at?

POD: Nothing, Mat. I just wondered ... I mean, you've had a lot of experience of that kind of thing; all those years thinking about it. Whereas I've never thought about it in my life, I wouldn't have the imagination for it; I mean, it is rather unlikely, isn't it? Mat, it wasn't a disappointment, was it? It did come up to expectation?

MAT: Shut up.

POD: Didn't it?

MAT: It was all right!

POD: *I* thought it was. Poor old Mat.

MAT: Shut up!

POD: Maybe it'll be better next time —

MAT: Shut up or I'll kill you.

[*Pause.*]

POD: I was up in the stars.

MAT: Where?

POD: Up in the stars. Didn't you get that?

MAT: You're lying.

POD: No I'm not. After she tied herself to me — did you see that, the way she tied herself to me? To *me*. And her eyes saying: 'I'm yours, I give myself to you, I belong to you, take me.' Strange about those eyes, strangely familiar, long remembered, or unremembered. 'It's all right,' they said, 'there's nothing to worry about, nothing can hurt you now, you're safe.' And into those eyes I sank like a child ... I've never owned anything before.

MAT: You're lying. It wasn't like that. You're lying.

POD: Didn't you get any of that?

[MAT *throws himself on* POD *as best he can for his bonds.*]

MAT: You're lying, say you're lying!

POD: You're hurting me!

MAT: Say you're lying or I'll kill you!

POD: You're strangling me!

MAT: Say you're lying!

POD: I'm lying.

MAT: You weren't up in the stars!

POD: I wasn't up in the stars.

MAT: It was the biggest disappointment of your life!

POD: It was the biggest disappointment of your life.

MAT: *Your* life!

POD: *My* life!

MAT: All right then.

[MAT *gets off him.*]

POD: All the same —

MAT: Enough about it! Enough of your obsessions. There are other things in life than that. My God, why am I cursed with fraternal feelings?

POD: Are you?

MAT: Why else do you think I've spent my life trailing you around like an everlasting turd on my shoe? Protecting you; letting you hold me back; cramp my style. Do you know where I might be if it wasn't for you?

POD: No, Mat.

MAT: No, of course you don't. I've limited myself, so you could keep up with me. Sacrificed myself. Left my potential unrealised, kept my eyes to the ground. No more. I'm past all that now. You're on your own, you can fend for yourself for a change. Get these things untied, go on. I'm sick of it. Get off, get out. I want to realise myself. I want to be alone.

POD: Hasn't done you much good, has it?

MAT: I said enough about that. I've got better things to think about.

POD: I'm sure you did your best —

MAT: I'll kill you in a minute.

> [*Pause.* POD *tries to loosen the bonds.*]

POD: Can you bring your arm over . . .

MAT: No!

POD: I'm going to anyway.

MAT: Going to what?

POD: As soon as we get untied from each other. Leave you.

MAT: Are you mad?

POD: No.

MAT: What would you do without me? I'll tell you, nothing. You'd die. You're incompetent.

POD: I may be incompetent, Mat, but there's one thing I seem to be able to — [*He catches* MAT'*s eye.*] Anyway, I'll take a chance on it. With all due respect, Mat, I don't think I need you any more. The love of a good woman has made a man of me. I'm going to find that one and we'll go off somewhere together. That's my plan. So I won't be holding you back any more.

MAT: My God, they've fooled you then. You'll play right into their hands.

POD: I wish we had a knife.

MAT: Don't you see their game?

POD: What game?

MAT: It's as plain as a pikestaff.

POD: What's a pikestaff?

MAT: One, they lull us, gull us. I saw their game from the start. Two . . .

POD: Go on.

MAT: Two, they play music at us, break down our resistance, make us go all soppy. You at least, I was too much for them. Three, they take your energy away, suck our energy out. And when they've got us well broken down they'll enslave us. I've got their measure.

POD: I need a pee.

MAT: They'll be back soon. They'll play more music at us; work us over again.

POD: Do you think so?

MAT: Why do you think they've tied us up?

POD: So we'll be here when they get back.

MAT: Exactly.

POD: I'm not sure I mind all that much.

MAT: Course you don't. You were born to be subservient. You should have been one of them.

POD: I don't see anything subservient about doing that thing. After all —

MAT: Shut up and let me think. We need a counterplan. We need to get back on the offensive. Can't you get those knots untied?

POD: I'm trying.

MAT: Let me do it.

[MAT *struggles ineffectually with the knots.*]

No. Wait. Guile, that's what we need. A bit of counter-lulling. Look as if we're beaten, pretend we can't get free. That'll gull them. See if we can stand up.

[*They manage to stand up.*]

See if we can walk.

[*They walk a few steps.*]

POD: Where are we going?

MAT: Back where they are.

POD: That's a good idea. Then what?

MAT: We'll throw ourselves on their mercy. Be nice to them, be charming, put them at their ease. Then at the psychological moment, pow!

POD: Pow, Mat?

MAT: Get our own back. Free ourselves. Show them who's master. Wreak our will on them.

POD: I thought we'd done that.

MAT: Once and for all.
    [*He speaks to the audience.*]
    There's a quality in men women have always hated. That's why they knocked us all off last time. They don't understand it, it frightens them, it's beyond their comprehension. Rooted in the earth they are, stuck in the mud of physicality. Words like sublime, ideal, infinite, strike terror in their hearts. They see us reaching out, reaching up, beyond ourselves, away from the earth, stretching for the stars. It scares the shit out of them. They laugh, make fun of us. Grab us by the ankles to drag us back down to earth. Well, we can wait, we can take the long view. They can't see what's inside our heads. We can wait for years. We can wait for a lifetime. [*to* POD] Just let me do the talking.

POD: They don't understand us.

MAT: Shut up and let's get going.

POD: Right. Which way?

MAT: What?

POD: Which way?
    [MAT *looks to left and right.*]

MAT: One of these days I'll get this bloody island straightened out. This way.
    [*They go off.* KAY, JO, VI, SUE *and* DEE *enter from the opposite side.*]

SUE: He's gone! Oh, my love —

VI: Don't start that again. They'll come round and back again. They can only go in circles.

JO: We may as well wait for the buggers. Let them do the walking.
    [*The* WOMEN *dispose themselves gracefully about the stage.*]

SUE: I shall lie here where he lay. See, the indentation of his form.

KAY: You see what I mean.

DEE: What did they call it? In the old days?

VI: Love.

DEE: Nasty.

JO: Lying there . . . You don't know what you'll pick up. Is this where you did it?

KAY: Yes. Just there.

JO: Grotesque.

KAY: It didn't seem so at the time. One kind of falls into the way of it.

JO: Speak for yourself.

KAY: You would, I think, I do think so. Especially when the music is playing. In fact that strange effect the music has always had, that kind of languid yearning, does seem designed for something other than just sitting around feeling high. It takes on a meaning, you know, when there's a — one of those people about.

DEE: True. [*to* JO] You remember how it affected us —

JO: I don't remember a thing.

DEE: Not unpleasant, you say?

KAY: Not at all.

DEE: Hm ...

KAY: Do ask any questions you like.

DEE: In what way — ?

JO: Do you have to keep on about it?

DEE: In what way was it not unpleasant?

KAY: I don't understand.

DEE: In what way, in what way!

KAY: It's rather difficult to explain.

JO: Grotesque.

DEE: Don't you think you're over-reacting rather?

JO: I'm not over-reacting. I'm not reacting at all. All I'm saying is it's grotesque, which it is, bloody grotesque.

DEE: Not necessarily. Look at eating. Pushing bits of fruit into holes in our faces, and all the rest of it. You could say that was grotesque. It depends what you're used to.

JO: You want to try it yourself, don't you?

DEE: I'm simply trying to keep an open mind.

VI: Don't you think it's time we decided what we're going to do about them? They'll be here any minute. It would be nice if we could show signs of a little more intelligence than they do.

JO: Well you know what I think. We should have knocked them off when we had the chance.

DEE: You didn't though, did you?

JO: I didn't get any help, did I?

DEE: You don't need help to stick a knife in someone. You just stick it in, it's simple enough.

SUE: Oh my own own own own love ...

VI: Oh, do be quiet, Sue.

JO: Look what they've done to that child! She's off her head.

KAY: The same thing happened to me and I'm not off my head. Speaking as the only mature person here with my first-hand knowledge, I think you're all making a mountain out of a molehill. I said in the first place the poor creatures were only trying to communicate with us — in their own way. Well, I communicated with them; at least with one of them. At least — haltingly ... I admit they are incredibly stupid, and there's a reservoir of brutality which needs attending to, but I think I could manage to keep the creature in question in order, even keep him moderately contented, given no interference from the rest of you.

DEE: So that's your game.

KAY: Game? What game? I'm only trying to be constructive.

JO: I won't have men on my island and that's flat.

KAY: *Your* island?

SUE: Oh, you're all so stupid! How can you talk like that? You don't understand anything! I hate you all! I'm going to find him. I never want to see you again. You don't exist!

[*She runs off.*]

KAY: Anyway, there's nothing we can do. You can't get rid of them. So we may as well make the best of it.

DEE: A *modus vivendi* with a *fait accompli.*

KAY: Just what I was going to say.

JO: A disaster. A selling out. We were happy here —

DEE: We were not.

JO: I was.

DEE: No, you weren't. We tolerated it, that's all, this strange empty life, because there was nothing better.

JO: What do you want better? We had everything we needed, didn't we, we were never hungry, we had no ambition, we lived from day to day, there was no danger, no difficulty, no ... I admit it was rather boring ...

DEE: Well there you are.

JO: Life *is* boring. That's what life is. Boring. What do you expect?

DEE: When the music was going you said to me —

JO: I don't care what I said when the music was going. I'm not responsible for the wind blowing the bloody tree-tops about. It's not *real*, is it, how we feel when the music plays. This is real; and it's boring, I admit, and I'm not complaining, and if it's a choice between boring and grotesque I'll choose boring; and one of these days I'll climb up those trees and cut their bloody tops *off*, and we won't spend any more time pretending life isn't what it is, which is boring. That's all I've got to say. Bring the men on, there's nothing we can do about it. Let the wind play in the treetops. Let's all go mooning about like Sue or dance around giving flowers to each other. It won't fool me. I'd prefer to live life like it is. Boringly.

[*Pause.*]

DEE: Right.

VI: When I first came across those two down on the beach, they looked so vulnerable, so sad, like lost exhausted children fallen asleep crying, that a lump came into my throat. And even while I remembered all I knew about them I still thought: 'Perhaps this is the real truth of men, this that I see now, the child, the lost child, perhaps men are children really, lost from their mother, alone, finding the world too big for them; they puff out their chests, brandish little fists at the world which frightens them so much, while underneath a lost child cries for its mother. Poor lambs; how they strain to keep that shell, that fiction of fearless defiance, when all they really want is to be reassured and comforted.' And instead of pulling them into the sea I left them where they were. It isn't their brute strength, you see, which is their best weapon, but their weakness, their vulnerability, their fear, their hurt. That's what they'll play us with. We'll learn to regulate ourselves to their needs, poor lambs, learn to play to their jealousies and fears. We shall watch while they set about making the world they fear so much safe for themselves and, they'll say, for us; pulling its fangs, controlling it, making it useful to them, setting everything in its place. We shall humour them, be ready with food for them when they come home sweating from their work; and though we may begin to notice that for all the work and ruin they do on our world their fear is still there as much as ever, we shall not be able to stop them, because by that time we shall be regulated too to their design, adapted, made to tick and tock like clocks, set in their mad world as if in amber. And it will go as it went last time. Till we destroy them again. And they come back again.

DEE: Delightful.

VI: On the other hand, I think there is something else there, somewhere; I mean, behind the comedy of it, behind the dream, something, waiting to be found. All the evidence points that way. Behind the music. The music is only a dream, but the dream, distorted though it may be, is of something, something real, a real world . . . where all is beautiful . . . nothing to be rejected, nothing denied, only a consuming in desire . . . past and future come together in an everlasting present made of desire and fulfilment, desire and fulfilment come together, made one . . . nothing but a coming together, a making one, a desiring-having, a con-summation, a consuming, a fire of delight without cease . . . when the dream stops . . . Meanwhile . . .

JO: Here they bloody are.

[MAT *and* POD *enter, and* SUE, *hanging on to* POD. *They stop.*]

POD: Do you ever get that feeling you've been here before?

MAT: Shut up. Let me do the talking. Ladies: your obedient . . . your — abject servants . . .

THE END

RANDOM MOMENTS
IN A MAY GARDEN

Random Moments in a May Garden was originally written for radio and first broadcast by BBC Radio 3 on 20 January, 1974. The cast, which included a character removed from the stage version, was as follows:

PHOTOGRAPHER	Anthony Hall
SURVEYOR	Vernon Joyner
DAVID	Peter Jeffrey
ANNE	Julie Hallam
KATIE	Helen Worth
SOPHIE	Barbara Jefford
ANN	Elizabeth Morgan
MARK	Hugh Dickson
DIGBY	Denys Hawthorne
KATHERINE	Ellen Sheean

It was directed by Richard Wortley.

The stage version was first performed at the Questors Theatre, Ealing, on 9 June, 1977, with the following cast:

PHOTOGRAPHER	Tom Pritchard
SURVEYOR	Robin Duval
DAVID	Robin Ingram
ANNE	Jill Allen
KATIE	Susan Hulme
SOPHIE	Dorothy Boyd Taylor
ANN	Ffrangcon Whelan
MARK	Nevill Cruttenden
KATHERINE	Jenny Ambrose

It was adapted and directed by Larry Irvin.

Characters

ANNE
KATIE
PHOTOGRAPHER

DAVID
SOPHIE
KATHERINE
ANN
MARK
SURVEYOR

There are two areas: garden and sitting room. In the garden, the two girls KATIE *and* ANNE *sit as if posed for a group photograph. They may remain there throughout the play. The* PHOTOGRAPHER *may be an off-stage voice.*

PHOTOG: . . . Yes, I think you'll need to close in a little, just a little this way. Can you move a tiny fraction to the left, sir, otherwise we shan't see you for the lady's hat. That's good, that's good. Now let me see what I can see . . . Yes, now I wonder — could the two little girls sit together, do you think? Such a pretty pair dressed alike, it would be rather nice. Yes, if you sit there, and the gentleman behind, is there a chair . . .? Yes, splendid. Now, there's rather a cluster on that side. I think the little boy might come over to balance the picture . . . Is there room on the bench for the little boy . . .? Splendid, splendid. If you'll all keep quite still now, quite still, quite, quite still . . .

[DAVID *and a* SURVEYOR *enter the sitting room area.*]

SURVEYOR: The main problem at the moment is the roof. They can't do anything up there in this kind of weather.

DAVID: I'd better pray for fine weather, then.

SURVEYOR: Otherwise, as you can see, everything's progressing very well. They should be starting on the decoration next week or so.

DAVID: So when do you think we shall be able to move in?

SURVEYOR: Well, I don't want to be over-optimistic. Say the end of next month, God willing.

DAVID: And the weather.

SURVEYOR: Same thing, I suppose. Now, the kitchen. Have you both decided how you want it?

DAVID: Yes, we do want the pine panelling.

SURVEYOR: You do, good, very wise.

DAVID: And some kind of embossed paper on the ceiling. You know the kind of thing, Victorian-style pattern.

SURVEYOR: Fine, shall I choose a pattern for you?

DAVID: Yes, if you would. Sage green woodwork.

SURVEYOR: Sage green, mhm ... And the cupboards in there you want kept, dresser and so on ...

DAVID: Oh, yes, certainly ... This picture window's a great improvement.

SURVEYOR: Does give a good view of the garden, doesn't it?

DAVID: Bit of a mess out there at present.

SURVEYOR: By the way, I came across something in the cupboard out there, interesting relic; I think I have it here ... Yes, here it is. An old photograph. I found it under the lining paper. It must have been there for generations.

DAVID: Not much left is there? What happened to the rest of it?

SURVEYOR: It had stuck to the shelf; I prised it off not realising what it was and left most of the emulsion behind. Just these two little girls left. But I thought you might like to see it. They're rather a charming pair.

DAVID: Victorian.

SURVEYOR: Mm. Early occupants, I suppose. Perhaps a wedding group. D'you see the large buttonhole on this bit of coat?

DAVID: Such serious expressions.

SURVEYOR: It was a serious business in those days, having a photograph taken. None of your Polaroid snapshots; you just had to compose yourself and wait. Instant expressions put on for the occasion wouldn't do then. That's why they always photographed workmen leaning on their shovels; only way to keep them still. Been a standing joke about workmen ever since.

DAVID: Sweet children. Pity about the rest of the photograph.

SURVEYOR: The only survivors. You could cut them out and put a little oval frame round them, they do quite good repro ones nowadays. Some people like to keep a relic from an old house.

DAVID: It'll still have the headless body at the back ... And it might have been taken anywhere —

SURVEYOR: No, it was taken in the garden. You see this bit of skyline? It's the same, I checked. Anyway, I'll leave it in here in case you want it. Now, about this sage green, I think it might be wise if I show you the colour charts for the kitchen units before you make a final decision on that . . .

[*They go.*]

PHOTOG: Quite still now, quite still, quite, quite still . . . I'll count to five . . .

ANNE: Katie and Anne, two little girls. I'm not a little girl, though, I'm fifteen. When the photographer said 'Will the two little girls sit together?', I pretended not to hear. I think I can hear a cuckoo, but the stupid pigeons make so much noise I can't be sure. I wanted to stand, not sit, I feel more graceful standing. I felt right standing there. I inclined my head a little to one side and gave a calm gaze into the absolute middle of the camera lens. I willed myself not to let my eyes stray. I wanted to seem calm, and direct, and enigmatic, which is what I am. I've been called all those things, so it must be true; by different people. Granny Burridge called me calm, and cousin Harry called me direct, and Uncle Percy called me enigmatic. Uncle Percy gave me a secret which no-one will ever know. Cousin Harry is standing at the back, next to my mother because he's tall, and next to where I was. I kissed him once to see if his moustache tickled. It didn't. I forgot to tell him why I wanted to kiss him, he was rather surprised. I was too. It was an impulse. I believe in obeying one's impulses. I don't, often, but I believe one should. I *have* been kissed by men with moustaches, but they've been old and a long moustache is different, especially when accompanied by a beard. Not that my father is old. Old*er*. I asked Cousin Harry, when he began to grow his moustache, whether he hadn't a more *adequate* way of indicating his maturity than by growing *hairs* under his nose. Then I suddenly spoilt it all by blushing. I don't know why. I never blush, I hate blushing. If he'd teased me about it it might have been better, but he pretended not to notice, so I had to as well. I suppose he thought he was being gall*ant*. To pay him out for seeing me blush, next time we met I spent the entire time staring at his ridiculous moustache. I sat opposite him so that our knees almost touched, and asked him questions about history, which he's supposed to be good at. Well, he is good at it, better than Miss Peake, who's a wrinkled spinster and obviously knows nothing of life except from books. When Miss Peake gave us notes on King Henry the Eighth and his numerous marriages I found it really rather grotesque; I darted a glance round the class, but no-one else seemed to find it anything but normal, not even Alice Appleby, who told me the headmistress once told *her* she was too grown up for her own good. She was flattered; I'd have been. Cousin Harry was suspicious at first, he thought I was teasing him about his pet subject, but I played the earnest seeker after pearls of wisdom, I'm quite a good actress. And as he got into his stride with the *real* causes of the restoration of the monarchy in sixteen what-ever-it-was, I gazed fixedly at his upper lip, until his voice began to falter, because he realised I was doing something and didn't know what. I willed myself not to look once at his eyes, and I managed it. And, also, I learnt that you can find out much more about someone by looking at their mouth than by looking at their eyes, in spite of what people say. Eyes don't tell you anything, contrary to popular belief, they are an inexpressive feature, they can cry or look tired, or squint in the sun, and that's about all; it's true, I've tried it with Katie, covering all her face except her eyes, I couldn't even tell if she were smiling or not. But a mouth changes all the time; people are given away by their mouths. I've noticed that since. Perhaps that's *why* we're

told to look each other in the eye, so that we won't
give each other away. And perhaps that's why men
wear moustaches and beards, to cover themselves
up. I learnt something about Cousin Harry by
gazing fixedly at his mouth, which his moustache
is too immature to cover. I learnt he's shy. All this I
worked out for myself, learnt it and put it together.
Not from books, from life. Uncle Percy gave himself away. Now he can never be honest with me
again. He has to treat me like a child, and I have to
act like one. How still we all are; how still.

KATIE: I think there's a fly on the back of my hand.
Walking. I can't look down. I can't even flap my
hand or swat it, or I shall come out blurred and I'll
get the blame for spoiling the photograph. 'Anne
sat still, see how still Anne sat, why couldn't you sit
still like everyone else?' Well, I can. I don't want to
be called Katie fidget whenever they show it to
anyone. I can just imagine, how awful. I'd go
through the whole of my life with it. The perfect
photograph in memory of the wedding of *dear*
Emily — where is she now, why isn't she in the
photograph, it's her wedding? — only there in the
corner, *little* Katie all blurred. 'What a fidget, Katie
fidget, she always was a fidgety child.' I wonder if
Georgie will fidget. They've sat Georgie on the
other side. He was standing behind me, he put his
bony chin on my shoulder-blade and moved it
about, it hurt, I told him to get off. I'd have
shrugged my shoulder up only I was afraid he'd bite
his tongue. That was considerate of me, only
nobody will know, I wonder if I'll ever get credit for
it, in Heaven, perhaps. And anyway, if he'd cried
I'd have got the blame, because I'm older and
should know better. Anne never gets the blame if
she upsets *me*. I'm pig in the middle. One day I
shall be grown up. I shall be as old as Anne, and
then as old as Emily and get married, and then as
old as my mother with children, and then as old as

Granny Burridge, and then I shall die, like
Grandad Burridge and Granny Filkins. And Bertie.
I'm eleven. Bertie would be thirteen. Anyway, I
didn't want Georgie's monkeyface next to mine, he
always looks funny in photographs. Georgie had to
go to the other side to balance the picture. I suppose
otherwise it would fall over or something. Silly
way of putting it, balance, balance is for weight not
pictures. He'll probably crack the lens. He's sitting
next to Uncle Simon and Aunt Mabel. Uncle
Simon came back from Canada. He wears an
American hat. He only does up the top button of his
coat, but Uncle Percy does all his up, all the way
down. Uncle Simon's waistcoat stretches tight
when he sits down, it looks as if the buttons are
going to fly off. He wasn't fat when he came back,
Georgie spilt something down his front, I don't
know what it was, my mother was ages trying to get
it off so that it wouldn't show in the photograph. It
would be more typical if it did. I hope this fly
shows, but I don't suppose it will. My hands are
folded, one on the other, as I've been taught. I'm
wearing a large hat. I'm looking, looking, looking
at the camera. This picture will last for ever. But I
shall die.

[DAVID *enters with a dish of peanuts. He
puts them down.* SOPHIE *enters.*]

SOPHIE: Zip me up, darling.
DAVID: My word, is that the new dress?
SOPHIE: Mm. Like it?
DAVID: Very much. It suits you. I like the neck.
SOPHIE: Not too severe? It's the new line.
DAVID: Very elegant.
[*He zips her up.*]
SOPHIE: Is there a hook at the top?
DAVID: No. Should there be?
SOPHIE: Not if there isn't.
DAVID: Why do they put them on, anyway? Isn't a zip
enough?

SOPHIE: They're to stop lascivious drunks making nuisances of themselves at parties. Drunks can't manage hooks and eyes.

DAVID: Is that a fact?

SOPHIE: Try it. Ashtrays, we need ashtrays . . .

DAVID: I suppose when women are liberated we'll need them at the top of our flies.

SOPHIE: When women are liberated there'll be no need.

DAVID: Hm?

SOPHIE: Oh, *damn*.

DAVID: What?

SOPHIE: Brand new, straight from the shop, terribly expensive. And the hem's down, look. The stitching's gone. Bugger and sod.

DAVID: You'd better take it back tomorrow and complain.

SOPHIE: I'm tired of complaining about shoddy things. It means going all the way into town . . .

DAVID: Ring them up, get them to fetch it. It's their responsibility.

SOPHIE: They won't, darling.

DAVID: Course they will, if you swear at them.

SOPHIE: Anyway, it's not worth it. And anyway, it doesn't help me now, does it? It really is too bad. I shall have to tack it up, and they'll be here in half an hour, and I haven't skinned the peaches.

DAVID: I'll pin it. Have you got a pin?

SOPHIE: It'll show if you pin it.

DAVID: No it won't. Give me a safety pin.

SOPHIE: I haven't got a safety pin.

DAVID: Hold on, I've got one in my pocket. Stand straight.

SOPHIE: What are you doing with pins in your pocket? You're like a small boy.

DAVID: It was on the trousers with the cleaner's ticket; I put it in my pocket because I don't know where you put pins.

SOPHIE: I throw them away.

DAVID: You can't throw safety pins away, it's a waste.

SOPHIE: How funny you are.

DAVID: You should think yourself lucky. There you are.

SOPHIE: Let me see.

DAVID: OK?

SOPHIE: Thank you, darling. Well, do I pass?

DAVID: With a push.

SOPHIE: There's a spot on your sweater. Coffee or something.

DAVID: It doesn't notice.

SOPHIE: Put a clean one on, you've got plenty of clean ones. Or a tie. Wear a nice shirt and tie.

DAVID: It's a tiny spot . . .

SOPHIE: Well, it's up to you.

DAVID: Here, I've poured you a drink.

SOPHIE: Thank you. Cheers.

DAVID: Cheers . . .

SOPHIE: Don't let me drink too much tonight.

DAVID: Why not?

SOPHIE: It's not good for me. I get maudlin.

DAVID: I hadn't noticed.

SOPHIE: No.

DAVID: Anyway, it probably does you good; you can unload your innermost grief.

SOPHIE: Not with friends here.

DAVID: What are friends for?

SOPHIE: Ha ha. Not for that, or you'll lose them. What have I got to be maudlin about? A nice husband on a good salary, three lovely children out of the way, a few good friends and a lovely new old house. Oh, that kitchen, you don't know how I used to long for a kitchen like that. What an ambition, eh, for a middle-aged ex-graduate, to bake pies in a bigger kitchen. Why didn't we move before? David, why did we never move before, when we needed to? It's too late now, it's crazy. There's only us two and the au pair, we don't need this place, we could live in a single room.

DAVID: With the au pair?

SOPHIE: Without an au pair. We could eat out. We could travel — if it wasn't for your job. You could give your job up; we could go to the country and grow vegetables. We could live in a caravan.

DAVID: What about when the kids come home?

SOPHIE: Bugger the kids. We've done our bit; let them get on with it. All those things, all those millions of things I haven't done in my life. And all we could think of to do was move; which we should have done years ago. Why have we gone through our life doing things too late? Making do. Poking about in tiny kitchens. Getting next-door's records through the wall. That garden; we never got it right. We never finished putting that patio down. It's ridiculous.
[*She laughs.*]
I must not drink too much tonight.

DAVID: I'll write it on your forehead. Sophie must not drink too much tonight.

SOPHIE: No, promise, promise you won't let me drink too much.

DAVID: All right. I'm going to have another drink now, and I'm not going to give you one.

SOPHIE: They're not *here* yet.

DAVID: Give me your glass. If only you didn't —

SOPHIE: What?

DAVID: No, nothing.

SOPHIE: What were you going to say?

DAVID: It doesn't matter.
[SOPHIE *sighs.*]
Here you are.

SOPHIE: Cheers. I haven't put the olives out. Tragedy upon tragedy.

DAVID: You've got a lot locked away somewhere, haven't you?

SOPHIE: What locked away? What do you mean?

DAVID: All this stuff about your happy childhood — it seems very fishy to me.

SOPHIE: I *did* have a happy childhood. I don't understand why you don't believe me. I should know. Just because you didn't. I had a happy childhood, really happy. I'm quite contented with my life. I just get maudlin sometimes. It means nothing. It's probably the menopause. Meaningless.
[*Doorbell.*]
Oh, God, that's them.

ANNE: Emily was married today. Now, that's strange. You can say someone was married and mean two different things. For instance, Uncle Simon was married while he was in Canada; but his wife was still in England. It sounds like a riddle. It's the difference between the past participle and the — adjective. Emily was not married, and was married, and is married. Adjective, past participle, adjective. Language is strange. At school in the English lesson it seems so matter-of-fact, so cut-and-dried. In the dictionary, each word has such and such a meaning. But when I try to write a poem it all goes fuzzy. There should be a book which is the opposite of a dictionary, where you could look up a feeling and find the word for it. I'm full of feelings with no words to fit them. Perhaps that's what being experienced is, having enough words in your mind. But I heard my father say Uncle Simon was an experienced man — a man of experience — and Uncle Simon says almost nothing at all. I write in my diary most days, and now and then I write poems. I don't know why I do it. Perhaps putting things into words stops them from dying. I was talking to Cousin Harry about words, he was in one of his rare serious moods. He said something interesting. He said — It's gone, I've forgotten it. Yes, he said: 'Nothing can exist until you give it a name; but as *soon* as you give it a name, you build a wall round it, its name is its prison.' I understood at the time what he meant. Then he said, 'There's a paradox for you, my dear Anne,' and laughed. He often laughs when he's said something serious, as if it embarrasses him. That night I wanted to write a poem. I usually light the candle by my bedside and write it in bed, but I couldn't start, I couldn't write a word. I blew the candle out, and then I started to cry. I cried and cried and cried myself to sleep. In the morning there was nothing. Katie heard me. She mentioned it at breakfast. I got very angry. I said,

nonsense, of course I wasn't crying, what have I got
to cry about, you dreamed it, you silly goose. That
day I tore all my poems up and burnt them in the
boiler. They weren't any good. Cousin Harry is
seventeen. He wants to go to University, but Uncle
Simon hasn't any money. Not enough for that. I
don't think cousins are allowed to marry. The
camera lens looks at me but it doesn't see anything.

KATIE: How still I am. I think that was a cuckoo. Polly
Daventry said that cuckoos make their noise exactly
once every second, but I don't believe her. She
makes things up. She pretends to know everything
but she never gets anything right. She's teacher's
pet. If noises showed on photographs I could count
the cuckoo calls. I am sitting up straight, as I was
taught, with my hands folded nicely and a fly
crawling over them. Anne is sitting next to me, and
Uncle Percy is behind with Aunt Lotte. She'll be on
the edge of the picture. She's always on the edge of
the picture. In her dark shiny dress with her dark
shiny hat. Looking into the distance; as if she's
waiting for a train to come to take her away. Then
there's my father and mother, they're in the middle,
and then — who? — I forget, I've forgotten someone . . .! Granny, Granny Burridge, is sitting at the
end, on her wicker chair. She does nothing, she sits
and watches. When she's tired of watching she
closes her eyes. She'll be good at this, watching the
camera. If we had to sit here for half an hour she
wouldn't mind, an hour, two hours, all day, she'd
sit, she's got nothing else to do, sit watching the
camera all day long and come out clear as clear.
She's deaf. Sometimes people shout at her and she
pretends to hear. But she doesn't. Grandad
Burridge died last year. I expect he's waiting for
her. Once I tried putting my hands over my ears to
see what it's like to be deaf. Anne asked what on
earth I was doing. I couldn't tell her because
Granny Burridge was there. Though she couldn't

have heard. Then there's Uncle Simon and Auntie Mabel, they're both sitting down; and little Georgie. Cousin Harry, he's the one I'd forgotten. I wonder where Emily is. She was married this morning. They rang the church bells. You have to pay them to do that. She'll be married for the rest of her life. If Arthur dies at sea she'll be a widow. I hope he doesn't. Arthur is an orphan, he hasn't any family. He was brought up in an orphanage and went to sea. He's not in the *Royal* Navy. He's been round the world. He stands very straight and hardly ever laughs. I can't imagine what it's like not to have a family. Perhaps I shall ask Emily to ask him. I know where she is: she's upstairs changing her dress, because they're going away. For a honeymoon. If you put your hands over your ears you can hear your heart beating.

> [KATHERINE, SOPHIE *and* ANN *enter.* SOPHIE *carries a tray with coffee and some kind of confection.*]

KATHERINE: Absolutely splendid.

SOPHIE: They were quite good, weren't they?

ANN: Marvellous. How *do* you get the stones out without cutting them in half?

SOPHIE: There's a special instrument for it.

KATHERINE: You've got a special instrument for getting stones out of peaches? My God, what a sybaritic household.

ANN: You poach them first?

SOPHIE: That's right. Then you push this thing in and it kind of claws them out. It's like a sort of Caesarian operation.

ANN: And then you squirt the cream in.

SOPHIE: It's terribly simple really.

ANN: You're so clever. I'm always meaning to try these things but I never seem to get round to it. I don't know why. The days are not long enough.

KATHERINE: 'And the days were not long enough, and the nights were not long enough . . .'

ANN: What's that, Eliot?
KATHERINE: I've no idea. My head's stuffed with scraps of dead
           poetry, left over from my dreadful education. Like a
           poetical ragbag.

           'Whither is fled the visionary gleam?
           Where is it now, the glory and the dream?
           Our birth is but a sleep and a forgetting.'

ANN: I think I'll have just another of these.
SOPHIE: Oh, my God. I've just remembered a dream I had
           last night. What was it? 'It comes like a crow — '
           I've forgotten it, I've forgotten what it was!
ANN: I never remember my dreams.
KATHERINE: Have you ever read Algernon Blackwood?
SOPHIE: 'It comes like a crow and leaves like a thief. And its
           fingers are sand.' That was it.
ANN: Sounds like a riddle.
SOPHIE: I was at school. I was giving out prizes. I was due to
           speak, only this boring vicar was giving an in-
           terminable sermon about dust and lust.
KATHERINE: Dust and lust? Really, Sophie!
SOPHIE: I'm sure it was all very Freudian.
ANN: I love hearing dreams. What happened?
SOPHIE: Oh, the vicar went on and on about dust and lust,
           and the kids sat in stony silence, it was really em-
           barrassing. So I turned to the person next to me,
           who I *think* was David, and said 'trite night' and
           everyone rolled about laughing. Then it was my
           turn. I stood in front of all those eager upturned
           faces, all waiting to hear the secret of life. I had
           enormous self-assurance; I let them wait. Then I
           said 'It comes like a crow and leaves like a thief, and
           its fingers are sand.'
           [*Laughter.*]
           And there was silence. Nobody got it, this beauti-
           ful, beautifully simple expression of what it was all
           about. I couldn't believe it. I said again. 'It comes
           like a crow — '
           [*The others join in.*]

' — and leaves like a thief, and its fingers are sand'.
The kids were giggling. And I started to cry, tears
rolled down my cheeks, and I woke up crying.

[DAVID *and* MARK *enter.*]

DAVID: What on earth are you on about? Now, who wants
brandy? Ann, you must try those, I bought them for
you; try the little round ones, they're something
else.

ANN: Thank you, darling.

KATHERINE: Sometimes I think that somewhere inside us we
have all the answers, just screaming to get out; only
we never let them.

ANN: Answers to what?

KATHERINE: Buggered if I know.

MARK: I wasn't trying to put you down, David. I wouldn't
dream of it after you've fed us so well. I was paying
you a compliment. As dinner-table conversation,
what you were saying was very entertaining,
perhaps a little heavy to accompany the sweet
course —

DAVID: Isn't it hopeless? Here am I trying to broaden your
narrow horizons so that when you've retired from
your dull business —

MARK: But I don't want my horizons broadened. Leave
them alone, I'm quite content with my view of life.

DAVID: You haven't got one.

MARK: David, when I retire I shall grow roses, read books,
talk to people when I want to and not otherwise,
play chess, go to bed early, take baths at midday,
and go into a pleasant decline . . .

DAVID: And then what?

MARK: Then what? Then nothing. Then I shall die. What
else?

KATHERINE: Mark, really, you don't believe life is that shallow.

DAVID: Of course he doesn't. He's a poseur. He's as terrified
as the rest of us.

MARK: Terrified? What of?

DAVID: The meaninglessness of it all.

MARK: What all?

DAVID: Life, my dear chap, life.

MARK: I don't find it meaningless.

DAVID: What's it all about then?

KATHERINE: Yes, do tell us.

MARK: I haven't the faintest idea.

DAVID: Well, then —

MARK: David, if I knew the Second Law of Thermodynamics — which I don't — it wouldn't make a scrap of difference to the smooth running of the physical world, would it? What an arrogant man you are! Do you think the universe gives a damn whether we understand what you call its meaning or not? It'll go on regardless; so shall we. We don't have to know why, any more than we have to know the laws of gravitation when we learn to walk. Our job, David, as human beings, is the same as that of any other animal: to survive and propagate, which means earning a living, supporting non-productive dependants, and getting as much satisfaction as we can on the way. Meaning is a luxury, my friend, it's strictly non-essential. If there is a purpose in life I don't need to know; and if there isn't, I don't *want* to know.

KATHERINE: Yes, but . . .

DAVID: Brandy, everyone. Katherine, brandy.

MARK: Now you're talking about something I understand.

ANN: How are the builders getting on, Sophie? Nearly finished?

SOPHIE: I wish they were. The trouble is they can't get on the roof because of the rain so the house is full of them. Marching to and fro in their great boots, dust everywhere —

DAVID: Darling, they *are* doing what *we* asked them to. And doing it very well . . .

SOPHIE: I know, I'm unreasonable. We're very lucky, I know that. And actually I shall quite miss them when they go. They tell me all their troubles, you know, over coffee, I can't think why . . .

ANN: I do admire you, Sophie.

SOPHIE: What for?

ANN: Oh, coping so well. You always seem to be on top of things.

SOPHIE: Do I? I'm not, actually.

MARK: Anyway, you feel settled in, do you?

DAVID: Yes, I suppose so . . .

MARK: You don't sound too sure.

DAVID: I feel in a kind of a limbo at the moment, neither in one place nor in another. I mean mentally. This'll be our last home, you know, almost certainly; an odd feeling. We shall die here. And our past will be elsewhere.

KATIE: I went down to the river with Anne and Cousin Harry. I don't think Anne wanted me to come. But Cousin Harry said: 'Very well, my child, why not?' He often calls me 'my child'. Then Georgie saw us going so he came too. Anne said: 'Oh, if it's to be a *family outing!*' She walked on in front, hitting at the grass with Cousin Harry's walking stick, while he asked Georgie riddles. But then she stopped and waited for us to catch up, as if she didn't care. It's not really a river, it's a stream, it dries up sometimes. Georgie said he saw a fish, but I don't suppose it was. He got his feet wet of course. There were some creatures flying about above the water. Cousin Harry said they were mayflies. He said they live all their life in one day. They're born in the morning and die when the sun goes down. I didn't believe him. Anne said: 'Of course it's true, everyone knows that, it's a fact of science.' Georgie found one on the grass and squashed it with his thumb. Anne said: 'You are a beast, Georgie.' Georgie said: 'He's got to die today so what's the difference?' Anne said: 'All the more reason to let it live.' I don't know why she was so upset about one mayfly, there must have been millions there. If I only had one day to live I'd get out of breath. Cousin Harry's stick was given him by Uncle Simon when he came back from Canada. It's got a silver knob on top. There's something strange about Uncle Simon. Nobody ever talks about him going to Canada. I don't know why he didn't take Aunty Mabel with him, and Harry. He was away seven years. It seems very odd. I asked Anne about it but she wouldn't tell me anything. I wonder if I shall ever find out. A fly is crawling over my hand but I shan't, shan't, shan't move. I'm wearing a big wide hat covered in pink tulle. I'm sitting still; I think I'm leaning over a bit, but I can't help that. I can just see the photographer out of the corner of my eye. He's got a droopy moustache, like Uncle Percy's only longer. I'm staring at the camera. The camera stares back at me with its one eye. Uncle Percy is behind me; I heard him sigh.

ANNE: Aunt Lotte, Uncle Percy, Mother, Father, Aunty Mabel, Uncle Simon, Granny Burridge, Georgie, Katie, Anne, Cousin Harry.

SOPHIE: More coffee, anyone? Katherine, a little more coffee?

KATHERINE: Plenty, thanks, Sophie.

ANN: My parents were chronically unhappy people; for much of their lives. Perhaps for most of their lives. My mother, when she was dying — she knew she was dying — said to me: 'You know, Ann, I've lived sixty-three years and my life has meant nothing to me. I shall be glad to go,' she said, 'Only it seems so meaningless.' My father, too, died bitter.

MARK: Why?

ANN: He felt life had disappointed him. Tricked him. Cheated him. He'd accepted it, all his life he'd accepted his — unhappiness as part of the way of things. Only right at the end he rebelled. It was too late. He lay there swearing. Died swearing at the pain, the final imposition on him. Swearing at his life. Lay there writing his life off with swearing.

KATHERINE: It's absurd.

MARK: Unfortunate.

KATHERINE: Mark, it's absurd. We accept it because there's nothing else we can do, but we don't have to pretend we can see a logic in it. It's absurd, by any standard. To live an empty life and then to die in pain, leaving nothing? You're a businessman: would you think that a reasonable proposition? Would you buy it? Would you be able to sell it?

MARK: I don't accept your premise. Life's only absurd if it *has* to be like that. I'm not such a pessimist. My own life's neither sad nor unhappy —

ANN: Good for you.

MARK: If there's something wrong with people's lives, they can be changed.

ANN: Whose, my father's? My mother's?

MARK: Obviously not, now, but —

ANN: So what about them? What about *them*? Do you write them off as experiments that failed? Rejected prototypes? They were my parents, Mark, they were people.

MARK: Ann, your parents are dead. The dead are dead. Whether they were happy or unhappy makes no difference any more.

ANN: To me it does.

MARK: Then you must find a way of coming to terms with it. You can't change the past. It's your problem now, not theirs. It's a problem in the present.

ANN: And what's the solution?

KATHERINE: It doesn't matter about the dead because they're dead; and therefore it doesn't matter about the unborn because they're unborn; and soon we shall be dead so it doesn't matter about us? Is that what you're saying?

MARK: I'm saying we can't help the dead; that's all.

KATHERINE: Does that make them less important?

MARK: To us, yes.

KATHERINE: Because we can't help them?

MARK: They don't need our help. Do they?

ANN: Some years ago, when I was going to a psychiatrist, I put it to him: that there was nothing he could do about the past, with all his skill, about all those people in the past. They were lost. He could neither help them nor give them meaning. All he could do was help us escape from them.

MARK: What else do you want?

ANN: I don't know.

KATHERINE: What did he say, the psychiatrist?

ANN: I forget. But it was to do with me, not them, his answer.

DAVID: Compassion is all we can offer. After the event.

ANN: And what's that to them? What will the future's compassion be to us?

MARK: Oh, come now. Do you think we need it?

ANN: I wasn't thinking of our cosy circle.

DAVID: Brandy, Mark? More brandy, anyone?

[*Pause.*]

KATHERINE: There's an adagio by Albinoni. Whenever I hear it I cry. Sometimes I put the record on in the evening, when I'm alone, knowing it'll bring tears to my eyes. Why should I do that? It's pleasant, of course, in an odd way. But what strange use for sadness. And why sadness? For what? What do I grieve for? Albinoni? What's he to me? He's dead, he should grieve for us.

MARK: What do you mean by that?

KATHERINE: I don't know.

DAVID: I took Eloise to see a film. She was quite young then, fifteen or sixteen. It was a very beautiful film, very moving. As we came out of the cinema I asked her if she'd enjoyed it. She burst into tears. She meant yes. She was crying bitterly, as if she'd lost something.

MARK: The nameless yearnings of adolescence.

DAVID: Why should she cry, though, with her life ahead of her? She was crying as if she'd already lost it, whatever it was. More brandy; Ann, more brandy.

MARK: Sophie: you're very quiet.

ANNE: Cousin Harry was coming to stay Sunday with us,

with his parents. But they arrived without him.
They said he had some reading to do for an
examination. I couldn't see why he couldn't take
one day off. Aunt Mabel said: 'He has no respect for
Sunday, but then I've no influence on him of
course, and nobody else bothers.' She pressed her
lips together, Uncle Simon didn't say anything, he
tried to pretend he hadn't heard, and looked
embarrassed. My father took him into the garden to
look at the shrubs; he's my father's younger
brother. I could see them through the window;
Uncle Simon was standing with his head down and
his arms hanging loose as if they didn't belong to
him. I'm sure they weren't talking about shrubs.
Something seemed wrong. I was angry. Aunt Mabel
was saying something about how I'd filled out; I
felt as if she were accusing me of something. I
wandered into the kitchen, but Katie and Georgie
were in there teasing each other. I felt I wasn't
wanted in the garden. I knew if I went up to my bedroom I'd cry or break something. I stood in the
passage. I heard my mother and Aunt Mabel
coming out. I ran to the front door and opened it
and went out to the gate. I felt suffocated. And there
was Cousin Harry, running along the road towards
the house. He said: 'How nice of you to wait for
me.' I said: '*We* heard you weren't coming, have
you changed your mind?' He said my mother's food
was too good to resist. I asked him why he'd been
running. He said he'd felt like it. His face was red
and shiny. We stood there on each side of the front
gate. The sun was out. He'd taken his hat off. I took
it and put it on. I thought he'd try and get it back
but he didn't. He looked solemnly at me. As soon as
I caught his eyes they slid away, as they always do.
We went in. I had the giggles. His mother made a
fuss of course, as if he'd put everybody out by
deciding to come; he gave me a sidelong glance as if
we were conspirators. After we'd eaten I said I

thought I'd go for a walk. Cousin Harry said he'd come too. I wanted to ask him about his father; I'd never had the courage before. Just as we were leaving, Katie came out and asked where we were going. I said: 'For a quiet walk', hoping that would put her off. But she asked if she could come. Then Georgie appeared. I said: 'Oh, if it's going to be a *family outing!*' Georgie looked upset. Cousin Harry said: 'Yes, of course you can come.' I went on ahead. But they were so slow I waited for them. We walked down to the stream. I was angry, I don't know why. My mother would say it was one of my moods. Georgie was very irritating. I shouted at him. I hardly said a word on the way back. Cousin Harry talked, but I didn't answer. After tea I went up to my room. I was lying there feeling sorry for myself when I remembered what the date was: April the twenty-ninth. That was the date Bertie died. He was eight. Georgie is eight. I felt wretched. I tried to cry, but I couldn't. I remembered my mother crying when she told me Bertie had been — I forget what she called it; 'taken away', I think; and I tried to think of little Bertie's face, but I couldn't remember it, it wouldn't come, all I could see was Georgie's. I thought: 'This has been a wasted day, a day wasted out of my life. Do I have enough days, to waste them like this?' I went downstairs. Cousin Harry had gone home.

[*The guests are standing, leaving,* ANN *goes out, or is out.* KATHERINE *and* SOPHIE *are talking together.*]

MARK: Now, where do you keep coats in this house?
DAVID: They're in the back room. We haven't got any —
MARK: I'll get them. I suppose Ann's gone for her last pee. She always has to have a last pee, she pees like the fountains of Rome.
DAVID: You know what it means, she's insecure.
MARK: Her bladder is.

DAVID: No, she's marking out friendly territory as animals do. Compulsive pee-ers are afraid of losing their friends. She's not peeing, she's beating the bounds.

MARK: Spare me the psychiatry.

[MARK *goes out, with* DAVID.]

SOPHIE: The fact is, I'm a little scared.

KATHERINE: What of, Sophie?

SOPHIE: I don't quite know. Finding myself with no excuses left.

KATHERINE: For what?

SOPHIE: For not doing what I want. For not enjoying my time. For not finding some justification for my old age, I suppose, when it comes.

KATHERINE: What do you want to do?

SOPHIE: That's just it: I don't know. I've lost direction somehow, I've lost touch with what I want. When I think back to my childhood, it was all so straightforward, there was a directness, a simplicity . . .

KATHERINE: Naturally.

SOPHIE: No, but do we have to lose it? Why should we? When I was young my wants were immediate, they came from inside me. Then something happened. The world began to press in on me, as it does, make its own demands, perhaps I gave way too easily. The externals took over, that voice from inside became fainter. Passing examinations, putting on a good exterior, pleasing a husband, looking after the kids, keeping the place nice — for somebody else, always for somebody else. I gave way, I suppose, to outside demands. Somewhere along the line I gave over the controls; I came down from the bridge into the engine-room.

[KATHERINE *laughs.*]

That's not a bad way of putting it. I'm a coal shoveller; I sweat below-decks to keep the ship going. I don't know why I do it, I don't know where I'm going, nobody tells me, if I ask the question I'm met with blank looks. What business is that of the stoker? And in a way it's true; if you don't know where you want to go, what does it matter where you're going? I've lost, you see, Katherine, I've lost contact with my desires; or perhaps the desires have gone, there's just a kind of yearning, a sadness where they used to be. But the result is, I honestly don't see the necessity of living at the moment. Not that I'm unhappy, I'm not really unhappy; not even that. I simply don't see the necessity. Isn't that awful?

KATHERINE: I don't think many of us could put it into words —

SOPHIE: I don't *want* to put it into words. I don't want to have to put it into words. A new born babe can't put into words what it's doing here, but my God it wants to stay. It wants to stay!

[DAVID *and* MARK *enter, with coats.*]

MARK: Katherine, this must be yours.

[ANN *comes in.*]

Have a good pee, did you, darling?

ANN: What's funny about visiting the toilet?

MARK: David thinks you do it for security.

ANN: I do it for relief, David. Goodbye, it was a lovely evening.

MARK: Marvellous food. Goodbye. And if you need any help, just let me know.

ANN: What, wallpapering?

MARK: I was thinking of administrative problems.

SOPHIE: Goodbye. Goodbye, Ann.

DAVID: Goodbye, you two. Take care.

MARK: I always take care. Goodbye.

[*Kisses and goodbyes, to* DAVID, SOPHIE *and* KATHERINE. ANN *and* MARK *leave.*]

KATHERINE: Come round and have coffee one morning, Sophie, we can have a proper chat. I've been meaning to mention it. We don't see enough of each other lately.

SOPHIE: I'd like that.

DAVID: Goodbye, Katherine.

KATHERINE: 'Bye. Look after each other. There aren't many of us left.

[KATHERINE *goes.*]

DAVID: Well, that went well.

SOPHIE: It did, didn't it?

DAVID: Small drink before bed?

SOPHIE: Why not?

DAVID: Come on, then.

[DAVID *pours drinks.*]

Food was splendid.

SOPHIE: Was it?

DAVID: You surpassed yourself.

SOPHIE: Nice people.

DAVID: Odd way of putting it.

SOPHIE: Why?

DAVID: Our oldest friends. Makes them sound like strangers.

SOPHIE: They're still nice people.

DAVID: Yes. Here you are.

SOPHIE: Thanks. Cheers.

DAVID: Cheers.

SOPHIE: I wonder which of us will be at the others' funeral.

DAVID: Good Lord. What put that into your head?

SOPHIE: I don't know. It's interesting though, isn't it? Why should it seem strange to mention it?

DAVID: Not strange. Just . . .

SOPHIE: Bad taste?

DAVID: No . . . Just a bit out of place after a pleasant, successful evening.

SOPHIE: Yes . . . Do you think Mark was all right?

DAVID: How do you mean?

SOPHIE: For driving.

DAVID: Oh, I think so.

SOPHIE: You only think so?

DAVID: If he's not, Ann will drive.

SOPHIE: Yes. That would be a bit out of place, wouldn't it? After a pleasant, successful evening. If they crashed the car.

DAVID: Oh, darling.

SOPHIE: Only joking.

DAVID: Is something wrong?

SOPHIE: No; nothing.

DAVID: You're probably tired.

SOPHIE: Mm.

DAVID: You go up. I'll tidy up down here.

SOPHIE: Oh, no, leave it, leave it.

DAVID: You know you hate to come down to a mess.

SOPHIE: Maria can do it.

DAVID: She's away tomorrow, you remember?

SOPHIE: Then leave it, it doesn't matter.

DAVID: It'll not take me a minute.

SOPHIE: David, leave it, please, please leave it. It's not important. Put some music on, darling, while I'm finishing my drink.

DAVID: What would you like?

SOPHIE: I'd like the first one your fingers touch.

    [DAVID *laughs. Bach. Solo instrument, harpsichord? Goldberg?*]

    Where's that photograph again?

DAVID: Over here. What were you talking to Katherine about?

SOPHIE: At the end?

DAVID: Yes. Here it is.

SOPHIE: Thank you . . . Nothing much. The tribulations of growing old.

DAVID: Who's growing old?

SOPHIE: We all are, I suppose, in a manner of speaking. I'd like another drink.

DAVID: Are you sure?

SOPHIE: I'm absolutely sure I'd like another drink.

DAVID: All right.

SOPHIE: Pretty girls. So serious. Such pretty dresses. I was discussing how we tether our lives to external factors; and as they disappear, so we are gradually cut adrift.

DAVID: Here you are.

SOPHIE: Thank you, darling.

DAVID: You mean the kids?

SOPHIE: [*on an incomplete note*] Mm, the kids . . .

DAVID: Cheers.

SOPHIE: Though what of significance we find in the bringing up of kids I've never understood; intellectually. They only turn into us, don't they? Usses. Silly usses. Cheers.

DAVID: You sounded a little upset. Talking to Katherine.

SOPHIE: Did I? Yes, I suppose I was a little. I'm not now. I suddenly feel very comfortable. Isn't it comfortable? After guests have gone; though I love having them. It's like — you know — Christmas when the kids were small; Christmas night, after the noise and the eating and the entertaining of our parents; when suddenly they've all gone to bed, and we're left, having a last drink, in a room full of echoes: as if, behind the quietness, behind the moment we're in, the other time is still going on; rustling of paper wrappings, movements, voices saying momentary, momentary things one would think would be immediately lost for ever. And the Christmas tree, do you remember? How the lights reflected in those beautiful fragile glass balls jump and dance as the sugar mice and the golden nets full of chocolate treasure are pulled from its branches? So that afterwards, in the quiet, there's an extra stillness in the tree, a stillness containing all that movement; fragile, glittering moments preserved in stillness, kept safe; not lost. Not really lost. Look, David, look at these two little girls.

DAVID: They're sweet, aren't they?

SOPHIE: Sweet. And so conscious of the moment, so intent on preserving themselves. Look: how serious this one, how solemn. And the little one, leaning slightly to one side, afraid to move. But she let her eyes wander, do you see?

DAVID: Let me see. So she did. I hadn't noticed.

SOPHIE: And this is what's left of them. Their future is the same as their past now. Lost. Gone. All gone.

DAVID: Sophie . . .

SOPHIE: As for the others, whoever they were, they've gone completely. Stripped — off. Stuck to a shelf in a

kitchen cupboard. What a destiny. [*She laughs.*] I
wonder what we shall be remembered by. Who'll
keep our photograph in a cupboard?

DAVID: There's always the kids.

SOPHIE: Mm . . . You're not really going to frame it, are you?
This scrap?

DAVID: I don't suppose so. It was just a thought.

SOPHIE: Lend me your biro.

DAVID: Here you are. What do you want it for?

SOPHIE: I don't think I want pictures of dead strangers in my
new house.

DAVID: It was Carter's idea, really.

SOPHIE: The surveyor?

DAVID: Yes.

SOPHIE: Just the kind of idea he would have.

DAVID: Darling, what have you done?

SOPHIE: Put moustaches on them.

DAVID: You are a fool. Come on. You're drunk. Bed.
[*They go out.*]

KATIE: . . . Aunt Lotte, Uncle Percy, Katie, Anne, Father,
Mother, Cousin Harry, Aunty Mabel, Uncle
Simon, Georgie, Granny Burridge . . . And a
butterfly! A yellow butterfly is fluttering about,
round the camera, perhaps it wants its photograph
taken, perhaps it wants to live for ever. Oh, if it
could only settle on the back of my hand.
Fluttering, fluttering about, the only moving
thing. Nothing for you here, butterfly; go and find
a flower while you've still got time. But it doesn't
go. What does it want? It's teasing us, laughing at
us sitting here so solemnly. I follow it with my eyes
until it's gone, gone, gone.

[SOPHIE, KATHERINE *and* ANN *come into
the garden.*]

SOPHIE: It's a mess.

KATHERINE: Oh, but it'll be marvellous. So much space, so
much potential.

SOPHIE: We've got a rough idea of how we want it. We're going to start with a patio out here, we really are this time.

ANN: How's David on gardening, Sophie?

SOPHIE: Oh, well, you know ...

ANN: Don't I know. I don't think Mark's ever touched a shovel in his life.

KATHERINE: But your garden's beautiful, I always admire it.

ANN: We had a firm in, my dear, instant landscaping. Cost the earth. And we have this little old man called Adam, would you believe —

KATHERINE: Hundred and twenty-fifth on F. eight, I think. Now if you stood over there we'll get the best of it and avoid the builder's rubble. For while the camera doesn't lie, it doesn't have to tell the whole truth either, does it?

ANN: Oh, are we having our photy took?

KATHERINE: Naturally. Special occasion, isn't it? To be captured for posterity by my new Super de Luxe thirty five millimetre S.R., isn't it? Come on, then, let's get going while the sun stays out. Where are the others?

SOPHIE: They're discussing double glazing. Mark knows how to get rebates.

ANN: Mark always knows how to get rebates. I'll go get them.

[ANN *goes out.*]

SOPHIE: I didn't know you had a camera.

KATHERINE: To tell you the truth it's the first time I've used it. I hope they come out. Well, how are you settled in?

SOPHIE: Oh, settled in. Do you know what one of the builders said about the little back bedroom? He was plastering up there; I took him up a cup of tea, and he looked out of the window and he said: 'This is a nice room. You know,' he said, 'this is a room I wouldn't mind dying in.'

KATHERINE: Praise indeed. Here they come.

[MARK, DAVID *and* ANN *enter.*]

MARK: If I'd known about this I'd have worn my other tie.

KATHERINE: Over there, then. Come on, no larking. This is a serious business. David and Sophie, in the middle, please, as befits your proprietorial position. Mark, don't lark about, you're like a small boy. Right, now, where's that bloody button . . .?

ANNE: It was Emily's wedding day. We all had our photograph taken in the garden. Then while Emily was upstairs changing her dress the photographer said he had a plate left, so would we like one more? I was standing next to Cousin Harry. I inclined my head a little to one side and gave a calm gaze into the absolute middle of the camera lens. Granny Burridge creaked in her wicker chair. In front of me sat fat Uncle Simon with his comical hat: Uncle Simon who ran away to Canada and then came back again; and next to him Aunt Mabel, who took him back but never forgave him. I was sure I could feel Cousin Harry's eyes on me but I knew if I looked round they'd slide away again, so I willed myself not to. His hand touched mine, accidentally, and stayed touching. I daren't move. And then the stupid photographer made me go next to Katie. Georgie was teasing her; he was sent over to the other side. Uncle Percy gave me one of his odd smiles as he made room for me, as if to say, 'Nothing really happened that day, did it? You've forgotten about it, haven't you? It was nothing.' It *was* nothing. I wanted to turn and tell him so. He was standing just behind me. Next to him, at the end as usual, mousy Aunt Lotte gazed into the distance, Aunt Lotte who lost all her children and always wears black. My mother and my father stood in the centre. It was very quiet except for the birds. Uncle Percy sighed behind me. A butterfly went by . . .

KATHERINE: That's fine. Lovely. Now just one more. Ready? Watch the birdy . . .

THE END

THREE ONE-ACT PLAYS

Post Mortem   Brian Clark
Too Hot to Handle   Jim Hawkins
Sunbeams   Rosemary Mason

A collection of three modern comedies, each lasting 50-60 minutes in performance.

Post Mortem Set in the modern office of a business tycoon. Helen Ansty, personal assistant to L.K. Halpin, arrives for work one morning unaware that her boss is dead. She takes over the running of the office for the day with remarkable results. — A strong leading female role plus 'voices on the phone' parts for 3-4 actors and one actress.

Too Hot to Handle One day Suzanne discovers a cache of pornographic magazines in her husband's wardrobe. When he comes home from work that evening she confronts him with the evidence. — A domestic 'marriage-lines' comedy for two actresses and one actor.

Sunbeams Set in London's bed-sit land. A social worker, Frances, meets Louise who runs a call-girl service from the flat upstairs. They begin to examine each other's role and function in society and realise that they are perhaps not so different after all. – A play for two actresses and one actor.

Free catalogue available from:
Amber Lane Press
Amber Lane Farmhouse
The Slack
Ashover
Derbyshire S45 0EB